A Reader's Guide to
the Chopin Preludes

A Reader's Guide to the Chopin Preludes

Jeffrey Kresky

Greenwood Press
Westport, Connecticut • London

Library of Congress Cataloging-in-Publication Data

Kresky, Jeffrey.
    A reader's guide to the Chopin Preludes / Jeffrey Kresky.
      p. cm.
    Includes bibliographical references.
    ISBN 0–313–29253–1 (alk. paper)
    1. Chopin, Frédéric, 1810–1849.   Preludes, piano, op. 28.
    2. Piano music—19th century—History and criticism.   I. Title.
ML410.C54K75   1994
786.2'18928—dc20   93–42788

British Library Cataloguing in Publication Data is available.

Library of Congress Catalog Card Number: 93–42788
ISBN: 0–313–29253–1

First published in 1994

Greenwood Press, 88 Post Road West, Westport, CT 06881
An imprint of Greenwood Publishing Group, Inc.

Printed in the United States of America

The paper used in this book complies with the
Permanent Paper Standard issued by the National
Information Standards Organization (Z39.48–1984).

10 9 8 7 6 5 4 3 2 1

For Jobi

Contents

Preface

If by "criticism" we mean not the common activity in journalism but the more intellectual or academic pursuit as it is found surrounding the literary and visual arts, then the absence of this practice in the world of music is a noteworthy phenomenon. So laments musicologist Joseph Kerman in his book *Contemplating Music.* Perhaps this lack has something to do with certain striking and fundamental differences between music and the other arts, which are in a sense open to contemplation at leisure (whereas music will not wait for you as you think about it). Moreover, moments of music seem inherently less easy to describe in words than literature (which, after all, itself communicates through words) or visual phenomena.

This book is offered as a work of criticism akin to the variety of "reader's guides" to famous written works or bodies of literature. In hesitating to make use of the facilely parallel label "listener's guide," I am wary of the casual approach to musical material such a phrase calls to mind ("program notes" and the like).

"Reader's guides" are often found for works that seem to require them by virtue of their own innate difficulty—as if one needed a map to get through some very difficult stretch of land; and the Chopin preludes are not obscure in this sense. But we find such guides also for works such as the plays of Shakespeare. Here, we discover that blend of analysis (however construed or styled), opinion (ideally representing a generally informed, educated turn of mind, and not some idiosyncratic or overly personal opinion—although a certain personal approach may be helpful in the guiding process), and—for lack of any better term for it—"musings," that may accompany the great, complex works of literature and be the looked-for "companion" to the reading experience, the experience of remembering and integrating the work.

Thus, although considerable analysis in the quite usual pitch-specific sense will occur in most of the discussions of these little pieces, commentary of other sorts will also be found: aesthetic, historical—in short, just those things that would seem to make up the kind of sophisticated "music appreciation" that perhaps is the best equivalent in music to the intellectually oriented critical enterprise as it is known and respected in literature.

Such a companion to the Chopin preludes has a variety of intended uses. Like its presumed counterparts in literature, it can be read by the academically inclined music lover—though the heavy amount of technical information required to follow the analytic descriptions and arguments would call for a well-remembered college study of music theory through most of its stages. But as a direct adjunct to college-level or graduate school study, the book might easily fit into courses or seminars in analysis, in piano literature, or in the period study of the nineteenth century. Isolated chapters could well serve for adjunct analytic work in upper-level theory courses.

Finally, in mentioning the obvious corequisite to this book—namely a good copy of the score to the music—I come to a crucial difference between companions or guides to music and those to literature. The work of literature and the guide to it exist in the same medium. Not so, of course, for music. Returning to the phrase "listener's guide" may suggest that one needs only a recorded performance to complement this work of commentary; while a "reader's guide" might imply, once again, the score. Obviously, the *listening* experience and appreciation of the preludes is what is aimed at here. But, as implied earlier, the printed score is the only convenient form of the music in which it can be contemplated, consulted, and considered: moments can be lingered over, reviewed, appreciatively or microscopically (and I see no reason why these two ways need contradict); and the printed page can often seem to condense or summarize music, which otherwise, of course, takes its own time. The moment in music—being a *moment*—vanishes at once, and can only be remembered or repeated. At least on the score we have it there before us, perhaps as an aid to more precise and complete memory, and less cumbersome repeating. I argue not for the score as substitute for the music—any more than for the text of a play rather than its actual performance: but in both cases the text is surely crucially convenient if we are to think carefully about what has otherwise disappeared, or at least faded in detail.

As to the matter of choice of particular text for these pieces, let it be noted that although any editor's tamperings with some pure or original version of this music will have yielded a score that features elements not necessarily accounted for in these discussions, the result is little different from the combination of these analyses with any given performed version of these pieces, which is likewise bound to "interpret" the music.

Introduction

Through most of its history as a title of a piece of music, the term *prelude*—literally "before the game" and probably just that originally—denoted the intent of the composition as a precursor of some other, larger composition to follow (of which the prelude itself may or may not have been a part). Hence, it could establish the key, or the mood, or the style of whatever followed, and for a large variety of reasons. A particularly clear (and historically late) instance would be the establishment of mood (or, quite differently, the unfolding of major melodic themes to come) before the curtain rises on an opera.

Chopin's twenty-four preludes for piano, taken either individually or as a group, are quite obviously preludes to nothing—unless each is prelude to the next prelude. This may have been a historically pivotal situation—in the sense of its heralding a change in the application of this title, such pieces soon becoming "character pieces" in their own right. (And, indeed, one later comes upon like groupings of preludes from Debussy, Scriabin, Rachmaninoff, Gershwin.) But in this particular, and probably seminal, case, the observation serves to introduce us to a general understanding of these pieces. For if a prelude in the earlier sense is intended to establish a mood, and these preludes succeed *only* in doing that (in the sense of omitting the presumably more important matter to follow), then the whole notion of setting mood, of striking poses, is thrown into stark relief.

Indeed, emotional and stylistic mood is the very hallmark of the nineteenth century, the romantic style. The prior periods featured in some variety their own allowable moods, but the nineteenth century specializes in it—starting, of course, with the emotionally charged moods of Beethoven, and typified most simply by the feeling-laden world of grand opera, ballet, and tone poem. In the Chopin preludes we have twenty-four distinct moods, each in miniature. The group as a whole may stand almost as a summary of the imaginable mood types available to the romantic composer, a veritable museum of the expressive possibilities opening up to the composer in Chopin's century.

Taken as a whole, the preludes present each mood attempted, posed, considered, and then dropped delicately as the silence between the pieces ushers in the next, while also setting to rest the previous. So we find among these types the combative, the brooding, the proud, the tender, the skittish, and so forth: words being plainly inadequate, even in the introspective sense, to capture their emotionally concrete suggestions. They may likewise be seen as experiments in musical surface, in the formation of surface expressive of a certain frame of musical attitude or mind. One may be enigmatic, another despairing, another jubilant, and the like.

The question of the organic unity and status of the collection— are these preludes twenty-four pieces, or one (in twenty-four parts)?—is not just interesting, but perhaps unique. Clues to an answer may lie in comparison with other like groupings. Chopin himself, as any piano student knows, wrote pieces in clusters, the title—indicating a "type"—held in common. Thus there are the waltzes, the mazurkas, and so forth, where "the" ought really to appear in quotes, to cast doubt on the significance of the grouping as any more than a convenience. When we hear in succession a number of his waltzes, say, we experience one and then another of a certain kind of piece; they don't fit together as much as simply remake each other. Published together (although in many cases originally written and published in smaller clusters), recorded together, even performed together, they constitute a "list" rather than an extended composition. But the preludes, alone among Chopin's output (and published under a single opus number),[1] are a different matter entirely. There is, first of all, a key scheme or succession that makes the connections between the pieces both compelling and natural. It is instructive to consult first the key succession in the preludes and fugues of Bach's *The Well-Tempered Klavier*, another grouping that exhausts the twenty-four major and minor keys in as many pieces. Here we find each prelude-and-fugue pair a half step higher than the previous (a pair in the major and then a pair in the minor at each step, actually). The move from major to parallel minor may well be heard in "compositional" terms, as a shifting or adjustment of mode; but the move up is not tonal in any usual sense, keys a half step apart having pretty much nothing in common in normal tonal ways. In terms of key, these pieces seem merely arranged in size place.

But key successions that have compositional value—that is, that express in the large something grammatically coherent—make for connected, interrelated listening (which is, in a sense, what being "a piece" entails). In the Chopin preludes we have a major key followed by its *relative* minor (a more organic, less categorical connection), and then the whole pair replaced by the like pair a perfect fifth higher. (The first prelude is in C major, the second in a minor; the third in G major, the fourth in e minor, and so forth.) In both this and the Bach scheme, all twelve keys (twenty-four, including pairings with minor) will be achieved. But in the case of the Chopin, the route *through* these keys will seem itself "musical": the move into the next major key from the relative minor of the previous major key will feature certain automatic correspondences in terms of shared scale tones, chords, and the like. Indeed, these possibilities are not compositionally exploited by the composer, but seem instead to lurk under the surface, enforcing an even flow of convincing naturalness. Thus, after the second prelude becomes the relative minor of the first, the third, in G, will seem to treat the just-evaporating a-minor cadence chord as ii in a new key—and so on. The composer is, on the other hand, occasionally careful to emphasize the obvious tonic-triad pitch links that obtain between a major prelude and the next minor one (two pitches of each major tonic sonority being retained to become pitches of the new minor tonic): for example, special re-soundings of last notes as new first notes abound. The G-major prelude ends with two rolled tonic chords, B on top; that very B then begins the slow, piece-long treble descent in the next prelude. The D♯ that tops the final chord of the quiet No. 11 then rushes off in a new mood in No. 12; the lone C that begins the opening solo gesture of No. 18 seems clearly lifted off the top of the just-faded prior tonic chord; moods switch on the G held at the top of the E♭ chord at the end of No. 19 when No. 20 begins; and, in a switch as far as this sort of link is concerned, the *lowest* pitch that ends No. 21 reappears alone as No. 22 begins, and passes by step to the new tonic, to which it seems almost to deliver or transfer tonic status. These gentle connections have a distinctly "piece-like" effect on the overall flow of the preludes.

Contrary to this observation that the keys here essentially form a tonally significant *progression*, as opposed to the *tonally* arbitrary arrangement in the Bach, is the fact that normally tonal progressions—whether locally (within phrases) or in the large (across and among movements of a large piece)—ultimately accomplish an overall coherence, usually in terms of beginning and end points. That is, the keys of the four movements in a symphony will, considered in the large, expand upon something significant about the overall key of the symphony (started as the basic key of the first movement, restored certainly in the last movement, and not just challenged or departed from in the middle movements, but explored or expanded by way of keys that have something to do with the basic key). But the key scheme in the Chopin preludes just keeps moving on, starting with C and ending in d minor. So if it locally moves musically, it does not seem to in sum. This last aspect then detracts from the one-piece impression of the group.

Then there is the matter of the movement across the preludes in terms of moods. Again, comparison with a true multimovement piece such as a symphony, and with a group like *The Well-Tempered Klavier*, is instructive. In the latter case, again, we see no compelling balances or flows as the pieces progress (and with any other common-named grouping of Chopin, we would only hear each piece *repeat* the type of the previous, with minimal change in mood). In the symphony, on the other hand, clearly the moods present a picture of contrasts, balances, and so forth.

In the Chopin preludes we find the greatest care taken to assure that a piece of one stark type is followed by a striking and refreshing contrast, in terms of mood, length, scope, intensity. This, then, is another piece-like aspect of the preludes. (Often one hears subsets of these preludes performed in recital, and the listener may find both the key connections and the mood connections disturbed; the original ordering then seems all the more satisfying.)

Finally, there is the matter of motivic intermovement connections, such as one occasionally finds enriching the true multimovement works. Such connections may be so frank (as, say, in the fourth symphony of Schumann) that one may feel robbed of the full thematic possibilities of so large a work. But more subtly composed, they may be highly satisfying unifying devices (for example, the prominent neighbor-note motive found throughout the second symphony of Brahms, or the dotted-eighth and sixteenth repeated-note gesture in the first and last movements of his G-major sonata for violin and piano; such motivic consistency in opera is another case entirely, and functions quite differently, but yet unifies vast stretches of musical experience).

Motivic recurrences of this kind are lacking across the Chopin preludes. But a far subtler process is sometimes detectable. Consider the start of Prelude No. 2. After the slow introductory accompaniment, the melodic E seems to revive the sound from the top of the last moment of the previous prelude. It then moves on to D to complete the opening unit of melody. This pair was a prominent feature of the earlier piece (see mm. 5, 6, 7, 26 and 28). Its influence continues on into Prelude No. 3, where it extrudes from the opening accompaniment figure, and also from the melody in its first phrase. Perhaps this figure starts to fade now; but not before it is directly imitated by C–B (m. 5). *This* pair then echoes through the first four bars of the fourth prelude—only to be replaced by A and B (mm. 5–8), which pair precisely gets the next prelude started! Long and thorough acquaintance with the preludes seems to conjure such intriguing continuities out of the music.

I conclude, therefore, that the Chopin preludes form a quite unique musical organism, much like, say, the sense in which a society of ants or a coral formation is viewed as being simultaneously a collection of individuals and a super-organism of many small parts. If in such instances biologists can describe each ant as more individual than the cells or organs of one higher animal, but less "complete" than one higher animal, we can conceive of these preludes as occupying just such a middle position. Individually they seem like pieces in their own right, if perhaps too brief otherwise to stand on their own. But each works best along with the others, and in the intended order. With a symphony too we may experience each movement as a complete piece, which, however, benefits greatly by inclusion in and presentation with the surrounding movements of the larger piece. The Chopin preludes seem to be at once twenty-four small pieces and one large one. As we note or sense at the start of each piece the various connections to and changes from the previous one, we then feel free to involve ourselves—as listeners, as players, as commentators—only with the new pleasure at hand.

The preludes well reward study and intimate familiarity. They occupy a special place in Chopin's output, and are in the opinion of many his best music (alongside the large ballades). Considering the titanic status of Chopin in the pianist's repertory, and the central, representative role of piano music in the totality of eighteenth- and nineteenth-century composition, we can view the preludes, in their joint summation and advancement of the developing possibilities of romantic expression, as a beacon of the musical thought of their era.

At the same time, the large number of strikingly different musical surfaces presents a splendid opportunity for an equally varied experimentation in analytic and critical commentary. Therefore, in these chapters, the emphasis or even style of attention may vary from piece to piece. But also, it must be said, some of the pieces invite more scrutiny than others. There is a marked difference in complexity among them, and, also, in the apparent care with which they have been created: the collection is somewhat uneven in quality. A few of the pieces, of course, are celebrated. Some are truly great. But it is difficult to respond with depth or sincerity to those few that seem only roughly or superficially realized. Thus, this guide will now linger, now rush, as the music strikes the guider; but the reader may surely wander at a self-chosen pace.

NOTE

1. These considerations certainly exclude the lone other prelude, opus 45.

*A Reader's Guide to
the Chopin Preludes*

Prelude No. 1 in C Major

The rolling buoyancy and adventuresome spirit of the first prelude—so apt for this case of "starting out"—are due to the
wave-like motion that is heard both in the agitated one-bar
gesture presented in each measure and in the single arched
span which rises and falls over the course of the piece as the
smaller units accrue. The music can be felt to swell over the
first eight bars, cresting modestly at m. 5 and gently subsiding
(with the decrescendo) to its own starting level in m. 9; it will
rise again from there to m. 15, and then a slight fallback is followed by a continued push upward, to a climax at m. 21 (ff),
and a precipitous recovery back to ground level at m. 25 (p).
From there to the end the motion levels off and quiets down.
Thus the early swells are subsumed under a single, embracing
contour.

This is the shape of the individual measure as well. Beginning
with a single low tone, each next attack brings a higher note until
a peak is reached on the fourth attack, after which the motion falls
away.

But a careful examination of this small gesture reveals more than the simple wave form. The high note of the rise—in m. 1 the treble G—also splits off from the basic contour and initiates a melody by step motion to another pitch. This step connection—which thus distinguishes itself from the piling up of skips beneath it—is sometimes upward, as in the first few bars, and sometimes downward. When up, it helps bring about the larger rising tendency of the piece, and when down it reverses the overall motion. In other words, fused in the wonderfully compact one-bar formation are both melody and accompaniment, with the melody emerging from the background at its central and highest point, where it takes off from the notes that led up to it (the falling motion then heard under it and the second melody note).

Further examination of the one-bar figure reveals that there is a hidden strand in the accompaniment that cooperates with the melody by duplication an octave down: the second accompaniment attack (the higher, more audible of two struck together) in each case preannounces the first melody tone of that measure, at an octave's distance. It is then notated to sustain until connecting with the step-related tone at the end that echoes (actually, sounds with) the second melodic note above. Chopin's stem and beam notation calls attention to both melodic strands.[1]

A slight alteration in this melodic pairing takes place in m. 18. Here, and for three measures, the inner-voice version of melody jumps in on the downbeat. This added urgency surely aids the final push to the climax in m. 21, and aligns with the crescendo, stretto, and increased chromaticism. (The reversions to this form in mm. 23 and 25–26 are puzzling, however.)[2]

Now that the melody has become apparent, we can tweeze it from the tissue in which it is embedded, and observe its course more carefully. The first-measure melodic particle of two upward-striving, step-related notes repeats for three statements. The last time it succeeds in moving higher. Thus, the climb that will occupy the life of the piece seems to take time gathering energy for the task.

Meanwhile, four bars establish themselves here as a unit, for in the fifth measure the melody begins to descend: the rising step becomes a falling one, and the thrice-stated first element in the climb is echoed in inversion in mm. 5–7; m. 8 brings the fall down to starting level for m. 9—so that eight bars now seems a larger phrase size (in four plus four).

Eight bars more encompass the next, more ambitious cresting. After the repeating four bars (mm. 9–12), rather than turning down the melody does continue to climb (chromatically now), and so reaches a higher climax (and therefore later in its eight-bar span as well), the G in m. 15.

The turndown is modest here, only the most temporary regathering of force. In fact, nothing but the prior establishment of an eight-bar unit suggests we hear a division here. Instead the music surges forward (from E, the earlier high point, in fact), fully chromatic in its insistent rise now, pressed by stretto and crescendo and those inner-voice pouncings on the downbeats.

The high point in m. 21 leads quickly enough to a deflation so that by the time another eight bars are over, m. 25, the original level is regained. Thus, the eight-bar measured progress, inappropriate for the push onward, is abandoned while the climax is actively being sought.

Reflecting on what we know now of the earlier music, we can hear the period of calm-down in greater specificity. First, in repeating itself from mm. 25–26 to 27–28, the melodic action is slowing down. Further slackening occurs starting in m. 29, where two melody notes reduce to one, and the single measure now repeats for a fourfold stasis. Finally (mm. 33–34), no melody note is present, and even the accompaniment has lost its agitated, wave-like shape, here a single-direction and smooth arpeggiation. Even the last measure slows down the motion compared to the next to last, for all tones are sustained with only one new one added. Thus, from m. 25 on, the music has by stages recovered from climax into full quiescence. Then, these ending moments seem like the large wave settling into equilibrium. The melody in mm. 25–26 and 27–28 exactly rocks back and forth between the G–A of mm. 1–3 and the E–D of mm. 5–7 (the low and high of the first cresting, here quoted in summary form), while the C of mm. 29–32 sounds as a midpoint of rest between them.

Finally—and as a first reference to the harmonic life of the piece—we can note that G and E, the boundary points of that first arch, are just two notes of the C-major chord that provides the boundary notes for the entire journey. The restart in m. 9 is from G, and the small crest at m. 15 is another G. The settling note at the end is, of course, C itself. But what of the highest pitch at the climax? As D, it would seem to contradict this condition, and at its most telling moment. An explanation may lie in a view of the process by which this height has been achieved. From the slow revving up of the first three bars, through the growing peaks and turns back, to the pressure of stretto and relentless semitone ascent into m. 21, the line has steadily gained force, which now may have to bring it just *over* the top: that is, much as a cat will overleap its goal in landing on a height, the line may be aiming for a C, of which the m. 21 D is an overshooting. (Indeed, the chord there is of C, with the D a nonharmonic pitch resolving to the C that follows.)

The C triad is thus the conditioning context for the melody; but it is, of course, the grounding sonority of the harmony as well,[3] in the form of first and last chord and that at the climax. The key of C may well be an arbitrary (if seemingly natural) place to start an odyssey through all twenty-four keys,[4] but it has one way or another come to be associated with a certain simplicity, optimism, or affirmation (as in the finale of Beethoven's Fifth Symphony), and so if only for that reason it seems like an appropriate key for the fine mood in which the Preludes begin.

The harmonies that connect the opening and closing C tonic chords while also supporting the melody are easily followed, once we understand that, as a model, in each measure only one of the two step-related treble tones will harmonize with the accompanying chord. What that other tone is—and which of the two it will be—will depend on circumstances. Thus, in the first two measures the A's can be heard as neighbors to the surrounding G's over the key-defining succession $I-V_5^6-I$. But in mm. 3 and 4, the A and B are passing tones. As the C-triad interval G–C is the first link of the climb to be outlined (the next is by skip, to E, m. 5), and as the G's and A's alternate before managing to ascend, we can, in keeping with our view of the melody as something slow to develop at first, also think of the first two A's as "attempted" passing tones.

An F chord of m. 5 harmonizes neither the melodic E nor the D, but the D is less dissonant with it than the E, so, with E as appoggiatura to D, we can hear a d^7, ii_5^6, chromaticized in the next measure into D^7, V_5^6/V, ushering in the double measure of dominant harmony that brings the first phrase to a place of temporary rest and prepares for the restart of I at the new beginning.

Starting in m. 13 we can view both treble tones as passing notes, as the chromaticism is introduced to make the climb more aggressive. IV in m. 15 is announced by its own dominant, the V^7/IV in the previous measure. The tonic harmony at the peak is not fully stable. This stability will be won by way of cadence formula, beginning with cadential (tonic) $^6_4$, m. 23, converting promptly to V^7 and thence to the root position I that supports the third appearance of ground level and essentially remains until the end.

The climax chord is linked to its cadential inversion by the most colorful harmony of the piece, the diminished seventh of m. 22, which Chopin spells as common-tone embellisher to the surrounding C chords, but which can be understood more typically as $F\sharp^{\circ7}$, $vii^{\circ7}/V$, the V arriving in the bass tone of the C^6_4 that introduces it. The dissonant passing-tone B delaying the full diminished-seventh sonority makes the moment even more luxuriant.

Measures 25–28, repeating the contents of mm. 1 and 7, retain a stubborn bass C as pedal tone under the alternating I's and V's, a token of the arrival of the final bass tone in m. 25. Measures 29–32 are less readily understood. The treble suggests IV, resolving to I in the last sixteenth—thus a plagal confirmation of the already achieved tonic; but this proceeds over C and G as double tonic pedal tones. The ending area, from m. 25, features (only) all three primary harmonies, all of which have had their own tonicizations along the way (by way of the only applied dominants).

The closing gesture harmonically expresses the slacking off of activity with which the melody ends, as the I chord is now rolled out for us, fully untroubled: for the first time, no dissonant tone sounds.

The wave motions, in which have cooperated the melody shapes, the harmonies, the registrations, and the notated dynamics and other performance directions, have subsided, the buoyancy of the C triad now spent. But we find that the final sonority has yet the smallest amount of unrest: the top of the chord is its third, not its root. Although the chord is surely very stable, it lacks that ultimate finality associated with the "position of the octave" formation. This imperfect cadence condition is in fact a feature of roughly half the preludes (11 of the 24—and a different sort of blemish in one of the remaining 13 actually makes for an even 12 and 12), an unusually high percentage. To compare with another sample, open the collection of Chopin waltzes, and you will find among any adjacent five or six of them that they are all bound to end with a tonic note at the top of the final chord.

This observation can be added to our impression of organic unity for the preludes as a set. The waltzes are indeed self-contained pieces, and need to seem truly over when they each end. The preludes often as not end with a tiny touch of the incomplete, making the appearance of a next prelude seem both natural and desired, more of an ongoing larger music.

NOTES

1. But notice that his rhythmic notation of the under-melody is bizarre—though not actually atypical of the generally sloppy rhythmic notation in some nineteenth-century music. If m. 1 has six even sixteenths (three plus three for the two eighth notes of the time signature), then the second-attack G would have to last for four triplet sixteenths in order to connect with the A on the sixth sixteenth; but Chopin draws a figure that should fill an entire measure of $\frac{2}{8}$ and squeezes it onto 5/6 of his bar. He hasn't bothered to work out the notational requirements of the situation, and apparently hopes his interpreters won't notice.

2. And the rhythmic notation is again nonsensical. If, as some apparently faithful editions have it, the last note of m. 18 is to be struck on the fifth of five even sixteenths, the dotted eighth on the downbeat again won't do. And it is a good bet that a quintuplet is not even what Chopin had in mind. He may have wanted the first two sixteenths evenly spaced over the first half of the bar, and the latter three performed as usual (as found in other editions, perhaps correcting Chopin's odd shorthand of the situation). Even in that case, the downbeat dotted note won't work.

Musicians probably didn't think about rhythm very critically at the time these pieces were written; rhythmic demands made on performers by composers were relatively modest, and composers perhaps just assumed that readers of their scores would successfully guess at the intended rhythmic meanings. Needless to say, such notational informality would never pass in the twentieth century, with composers aiming at so much rhythmic complexity.

3. Before moving on to the harmony, we may note the control the C triad exerts in shaping the bass line as well. If we take the true bass line to be the succession of lowest, first tones in each measure, it will be heard to

follow a strictly C-triad-bounded path, just as the melody does. The B in m. 2, for example, though of course a chord tone of the G^7 we will shortly identify there, is just as well a neighbor tone between the two surrounding (downbeat) C's. We can then continue to diagram (and thus hear) the bass line as follows:

Once again, the boundary points, the goals, the intervals passed through, and the notes subject to neighbor elaboration are all seen to be C's, E's, and G's. It is an interesting exercise of ear training to perform this piece with the left-hand pinky notes artificially emphasized, so that the C-triad significance of the bass line can be heard independent of its role of underlying and controlling the harmony. Then play the piece again (or just listen to a recording) with the bass played normally, trying, however, to elevate the status of each bass note, so that the line that connects them can still be traced and felt as such.

4. The two books of *The Well-Tempered Klavier* of Bach start with pieces in C, as do his sets of two- and three-part inventions. The key is certainly no more basic than any other in the internal sense, having precisely the same inner structure as any major key; but it does *look* simpler on the page, and the C scale is, for example, physically an easier route across the notes than any other. Presumably, the entire collection of preludes could be rotated, with each piece retaining most of its unique character in a different key. The whole question of keys being mood specific is complex and speculative. Of course they differ in important ways—even if only in how they sit on various instruments (or, for that matter, in our bodies as receptors): witness the plain fact that composers do choose one key over another, even to the point of developing a vaguely identifiable "manner" associated with a given key. Chopin himself, actually, only very rarely wrote in the key of C major.

and in shape this last bit of melodic utterance reflects a segment of the theme.

Probably the harmonies that wander from the initial e minor into the eventual E major of m. 21 are not sufficiently directed to form a connection between them, so it seems unlikely that we can hear the opening e as dominant for the concluding a. (And it would be in any case a singularly lifeless dominant, lacking the leading tone—its third—and, thus, any sense of drive toward movement or resolution.) We don't even have much reason to hear the E of m. 21 as V of a. Similarly, it is difficult to connect the ending tonic to the earlier ("cadential?") a_4^6.

Perhaps one way to consider the whole is not that we may only questionably follow the grammatical connections outlined, but that the ending piously enforces an organization upon what has been purposely presented as not very well organized. It is as if a force—a kind of will—exerts itself at the end on the various, tenuously understood thoughts that are scattered behind it; it gathers them into a coherence and imposes order and rest upon them and out of them.

NOTE

1. Highly blemished to be sure! But the model for it is m. 1. If the low G♯'s and G alternate as neighbors to A, then the D–A fifth predominates, starting the measure and holding throughout. The ugly smudge caused by the G♮ over the first G♯ results from G lasting too long from the previous chord (suspension); in time it gives way to (chordal) F♯—which, however, collides with the G♯ neighbor sounding beneath it. Only on the last eighth note of the measure does the chord come fully into consonant focus. Its gradual approach to realization—it seems to drag itself out of the G chord before it—does much to establish the crabbed mood of the piece. It also strains our hearing considerably, as we try to make a D chord out of it. The clarity of D-major outline in the melody above is of little avail.

Prelude No. 3 in G Major

The gloom of the second prelude is readily dispelled by the rippling grace of the next piece. The surface activity may superficially invoke the pace of the first prelude, but the underlying harmonic language is much simpler, and, altogether, the sense of urgency is absent. Actually, the rate of chord change—the harmonic rhythm—is itself slow, which resembles more the manner of the second prelude. Thus, among the three, surface and subsurface aspects are nicely shuffled to yield new results.

Two initial bars of accompaniment harmony present a chord that remains under the following four measures of melody. The underlying chord is the tonic, G; but its particular form of gestural presentation introduces some central features of the piece. The initial and ending skips (across G's, B's and D's) arpeggiate the chord for us, and in between, these same notes form the goal points of step motions. The exception to this is the most interesting note in the shape, the E that is the high point and approximate midpoint of the line. This note seems to overshoot the structurally solid D (to which it is thus an incomplete neighbor), and gently obtrudes from the chord sound being unfolded.

This observation is immediately useful in learning to hear a lovely secret in the melody as it opens. For that melody outlines the same chord, with the same "bump" on it: that is, the first melodic statement (up to the large rest in m. 6) consists of G-triad tones (and their G-triad couplings), with the exception of the (coupled) E at the end of m. 3, which again acts as neighbor to the following D (both harmonized in thirds); then this feature is restated in inversion.[1] It is interesting to isolate this relationship, the melody's augmentation of the accompaniment's one grain of irritation; if one plays the excerpts side by side, the echo seems clear:

These ways of hearing, both chordal and linear, see us through the ensuing material. Among other things, we can now simply read the chords as they occur in transposition of the original complex (thus, A major in the m. 7 bass, D in m. 8, and so forth). We then discover a very simple piece-long progression, briefly tonicizing V (in m. 8) and then IV (m. 18) before returning to a final I (m. 26). At that point, and in direct reference to and balance of the opening stasis on I, the harmony remains with G until the end of the music.

Meanwhile, the melody progresses from m. 7 in a way also related to what we can learn to hear in the opening bars. The prominent addition of the melodic F♯, downbeat of m. 7, makes of the A[7] a tense sonority, in which the F♯ can be heard as a tremendously stressed upper neighbor to the properly chordal E,[2] itself making only the briefest appearance to resolve the F♯ and relieve the tension at the end of the measure. But this appoggiatura effect can be understood just by way of the E–D pairs at the outset: in fact, the "bump" figure in this measure's accompaniment is also F♯ to E, nested centrally in the wider F♯–E connection in the treble. Thus, the melodic moment can be heard luxuriantly augmenting the special feature in the bass.

The V^7/V–V pair of measures is repeated in mm. 9–10, but this time the V comes out as V^7, thus cancelling the momentary tonicization of V, and lasts through an extra bar (m. 11) in preparation for return to I and a restart of the piece (m. 12). Meanwhile, in this extra[3] bar of V^7 we have the addition of E (melody), a chordal ninth that we can hear in familiar (by now motivic) terms, referring back, by way of the treble E–D of m. 3, to the original added E of m. 1. (And even this latest E is followed by a D, which can resolve it.)

This restart lasts just four bars, the extent of the original melodic phrase; and now we turn toward IV. The change in harmonic direction is due to the inflection of I (G) into V^7/C, the G^7 of m. 16. This lingers for two bars, and includes an interesting melody pitch, yet another E, in the middle of m. 17. If we understand first the chromatic neighboring D♯ performs for the E's around it, we can hear the two E's as linked, with the earlier (dissonant) one then anticipating the later one, introducing the top of the resolving C chord a little early. (The succession F–E–D♯ may superficially resemble a passing motion; but if the passage is played omitting the D♯, and then again as written, the experiment may audibly clinch the matter.)

The stasis on IV now is impressive, exactly matching that on I at the beginning (and then itself to be outdone by the appropriately longer presentation of G again at the end). But a subtle and curious change takes place during this time of IV: the chord is of course unfolded and expressed in just the way of the piece, but in its last two repetitions, mm. 22–23, the descending passing-tone F is changed to F♯. The mild Lydian flavor thus imparted to the moment can best be understood as functionally significant: for each chord in this piece the matching scale (based on the chord root) has been used for its elaboration, and this is true in mm. 18–21 for IV as well (the C scale, for a C chord). But in m. 22 the replacement of F by F♯ results in the G scale as the source of the figure (still for the elaboration of a C chord). This may aim at slanting the C away from its local role as I of C and back toward its next (and overall) function as IV in G: for the immediately following D^7 and G chords do indeed make of the C a subdominant, for a IV–V–I rearrival in G.

It must be added that the effect is not bound to succeed. To make it sound one would have to assert the slight alteration from the previous repetitions by artificially emphasizing the F♯ above the surrounding notes; but this would be very awkward, given the note's weak metrical position, and the attempt would run contrary to the smooth, carefree ripples as they have otherwise probably been performed. Perhaps the F♯ must remain buried in the flurry of notes, where the careful listener may hear it, if at all, only as an anomaly.

Meanwhile, this long IV chord begins to underlie tones dissonant with it as they arise in the melody (B, m. 22, and so forth). One is tempted to hear these as successive passing tones in a slow descent from the C of m. 20 to the concluding G in m. 26, but the progress—which continues over the succeeding D^7—is a little indirect after a while, with multiple interpretations possible for some of the notes along the way. From m. 22 through m. 24 none of the melody tones fit the chords, and the little flip from B to G even anticipates a portion of the expected resolution harmony. What is clear is the direct anticipating G at the end of m. 25, patly announcing the resolution.

The full bar of silent treble in m. 27 exactly (and uniquely) recaptures the opening accompaniment, and the doubling in octaves that forms the little coda (in which the full figure is successively shortened until it rises into a kind of evaporation) carefully includes a touch of simultaneous harmony, the repeated downbeat treble B (over G); this effect seems to presage the imperfect I chord strummed at the end, where the third on top serves for the effect found at the end of the first prelude. The high B's that echo from the last of the rapid notes nicely reinforce this form of the final tonic.

NOTES

1. Actually "complementation," for the figure is not turned upside down, but inside out. Tonal theory has traditionally used the term "inversion" casually.

2. Or, across the previous silence, as a passing tone from G.

3. Mm. 7–10 match the length of mm. 3–6, the first phrase of melody.

Prelude No. 4 in E Minor

A central feature of this celebrated prelude is the clear division into two parts. The constant chugging motion in the bass accompaniment ceases about midway through the piece, the melody now wandering alone until the opening music is heard again (m. 13) in a restart of the piece so declarative that the whole is split in two. Restarts occur in the first and third preludes, but without the form-determining clarity assured by this cooperation of texture and timing. These two parts will be heard as housing a two-part story, an incompletion at the end of part one motivating the "second try" that leads to a successful outcome.

The melodic "noodle" of m. 12, basically an elaborated B-major chord over the B^7 that concludes the harmonic progress of part one, can very nicely be heard as an embellishment of the pick-up figure that opens the piece: that is, before the original melody and bass pattern begin, there is that solo rising B octave (prior to m. 1). Here in m. 12, once again in solo, the line wanders down to the same low B, and ends with the same directly anticipating higher

B, both moments yielding identical music that leads off with the so-given, long, downbeat B.

The opening gesture is itself an expressive one, handing us the higher B as if with outstretched arm. A slow, piece-long melodic process starts from this offered note. The B is at first repeated in slow, upper-neighbor embellishment over the first four bars, the C appropriately shorter and weaker. This prolongation of B takes place over the shifting accompanimental background that continually casts it in changing light.

In m. 4 the embellishing pitch is suddenly B♭, a balancing half step below; but this fulfills a new function as it chromatically passes the motion down to A, which now is repeated and embellished over bars 5–8 just in parallel to the opening presentation of B. Thus B, the fifth degree of the opening tonic sonority, gives way to A, the fourth degree, in the first step of a gradual descent to E that will occupy the entire piece, a trip spanning the limits of the tonic chord just as it connects the tops of the two end-point statements of that chord.

A little touch of impatience in the figure of m. 7 seems to prompt this dilatory descent to continue. And so it moves on, as G♯, accented at the end of m. 8, seems at first to sound in parallel to the B♭ of m. 4. But this proves to be no descending chromatic passing tone (as the accent itself suggests); locally it seems more like a lower neighbor to A, which arrives in the next measure over an unusually stable a-minor (iv) chord. This iv is elaborated in the melody, in a brief flurry of departure from the melodic norm. (This moment may prepare the way for the slightly more extensive such figure of m. 12, even reaching up to the same high point.) But when the line settles back down we are left with a clear F♯, $\hat{2}$,[1] now treated so as to resemble the $\hat{5}$ and the $\hat{4}$—that is, sustained and repeated. So we feel we are on track again, and can think back to the oddly accented (and sustained, though syncopated) G♯ of m. 8 to wonder if it was the hurried (and modally incorrect) third degree in a $\hat{5}$–$\hat{4}$–$\hat{3}$–$\hat{2}$ descent to date.

In any case, the $\hat{2}$ is readily experienced as the heir to $\hat{5}$ and $\hat{4}$; the note with which it alternates, however, breaks the neighbor-note pattern, being a minor third away. But the embellishment for B (mm. 1–4) had been by semitone, while that for A (mm. 5–8) was with twice that distance (this due just to the shape of the minor scale). In a sense, our neighbor form has just widened one more half step, yielding A as a kind of stretched-out upper auxiliary to F♯.

The second degree is as far as we get in this first half of the piece: and it is just this failure to reach $\hat{1}$, the tonic—in fact, just this quality of *almost* reaching it—that motivates the piece to begin again, starting with the same (but more elaborately prepared) B to attempt a full and successful descent into home. Meanwhile, the last four melody notes of part one would seem to be B–A–G–F♯, starting with the grace note of m. 11 (for these four notes surely embellish a last F♯–A pair, and then a jump from the F♯ begins the wandering that connects the two sections). Thus the progress of the melody of part one is summarized in its final four notes (a summary that incidentally corrects and clarifies the third degree). The figure elaborating the opening B octave now takes its cue from the G–F♯, dropping down a tritone to imitate (both half steps ending in tones of the present chord), wandering up the V chord, and reaching low and high points that capture and quote the limits of the melody of part one altogether.[2] The last B will serve to announce the restart to come.

Part two may start plainly, but soon gets considerably sidetracked. In m. 16 we seem to start to move downward with A♯, but a sudden flurry that picks up from and surely outdoes the previous two (which thus build up to it) interrupts the slow process. But as we come through to a clearing, in m. 18 (parallel to the emergence at m. 10), we find ourselves right back on the path, but advanced to the $\hat{2}$, F♯, the point attained by the end of the first half. The remainder of the piece will deal with delivering this second degree into the tonic. Another touch of impatience is felt in m. 19 (but also echoing m. 11), and the anticipation at the end of m. 20 finally ushers in the E, downbeat of m. 21. As will promptly be heard, the harmonic support for this important note is all wrong, thwarting any chance of hearing satisfying resolution here. But surely we will have time to fix the harmony, as E must now be treated according to the previous steps in line—that is, "established" through the typical pattern of neighbored repetition.

As will be shown, this harmonic adjustment itself goes awry by m. 23, so that by the time the E is played out, we are still unresolved, and the impressive silence keeps us hanging in this condition. The little coda to follow will settle those harmonic problems; but melodically it takes E and treats it to a balancing *lower*-neighbor embellishment. The final E is firmly supported by the longest chord of the piece, the only root-position tonic sonority to be found.

The melodic line of the piece is, with occasional brief interruptions, simple; but it is throughout complexly cast by a rich harmonic life. The observation regarding the uniqueness of the final chord can serve to introduce this harmony, for we do not find at the outset the customary solidity: the piece strikingly begins in an unstable i^6. From there the harmony is notoriously ambiguous, with many chords of no immediately recognizable function. The apparent move into V^7 (with suspended E) seems clear in m. 2; but then a long series of inscrutable chords appears; a variety of sonic types—minor-minor-seventh chords, half-diminished and fully diminished sevenths, even dominant sevenths—is further confused by frequent dissonant intersection with the melody note of the moment.

A way out of this interpretive problem is to approach these chords linearly: that is, regard the change from m. 1 to m. 2 as a lowering of the bottom two notes of i^6. The result can thus be not a new, purposeful harmony with a root function, but a i^6 distorted by downward stretch (perhaps *toward* something). Just when V^7 seems established, the bottom note falls again (to F, m. 3). The top chord note falls next (all sink by half step, as if the original e-minor chord were dripping away), and then the middle (A to G♯, end of m. 3). If we continue to follow in this manner we find the original bass chord comprising the beginning points of three pitch strands that mutually descend, uncoordinated, unsynchronized, staggered. These descents are perhaps imitative of the basic melodic descent, and we may consider these lines as seeking their next positions in the goal chord of B^7 at m. 12 (itself of course just a middle ground between the opening and closing tonics). These unharnessed descents yield—almost as if haphazardly—the whole array of chord types, which now by and large can be considered not directed harmonic statements, but rather the chance confluence of the three strands at any one particular moment in their separate but simultaneous slides downward. Thus, for example, the E^7 of m. 4 suggests V^7 of iv, but surely fails to act that way:

quite the contrary, the leading tone in it—G♯—falls (as it is bound to in this scheme) rather than rises (as it would in normal resolution to iv). Thus also with the D^7 of m. 7. Perhaps it is not that these lack function, but more that their functions are suggested, proposed, and then withdrawn, as the inexorable downward forces sap the harmonies of their hope of resolution.

Meanwhile, signs of stability begin to appear in approach of the ultimate V. The $g♯^{°7}$ at the end of m. 8 does resolve normally, to iv (B and G♯ are suspended at the beginning of m. 9)—thus, $vii^{°7}$/iv. This properly introduced iv is further stabilized by agreement with the treble, and forms in fact the first consonant sonority since the original i^6. From here we can easily trace progression into and out of the dominant, until the motion stops on the last B chord. The overall harmonic journey of part one is then marked by the three primary chords, i–iv–V.

As part one brought $\hat{5}$ as far as $\hat{2}$, it has brought i^6 as far as V^7, and the quest for completion in both planes must renew and succeed, which they now do.[3] Part two thus begins again in i^6. The initial bass descents hurry at first (mm. 14 and 15 as compared with 2 and 3), and then break pattern, when the melody does, resulting in the spectacular V^9 of m. 17, the loudest and thickest moment (whose dissonant registral extremes, B and C, may be heard to explode and verticalize the mid-register B and C found quietly side by side in m. 1). This burst of activity subsides into the V-seeking iv associated with the previous melodic "recovery" of m. 10—now at m. 18 (second half). V is repeatedly attempted (it must be restored before ultimate resolution to i, as the $\hat{2}$ is trying to find its way into $\hat{1}$), delayed by a stubbornly suspended E (out of the iv chords), and finally achieved on beat 3 of m. 20. This then intensifies into V^7 on beat 4, and, in harness with $\hat{2}$, all is set to resolve together. The appearance of the anticipating E at the end of the bar convinces us we are about to get what we have sought from the outset.

The occurrence of a C-major chord on the downbeat of m. 21, a VI instead of the expected i, is an emotionally charged deceptive resolution of the hard-won V, especially as it replaces a chord so long looked for, and so painstakingly prepared over the previous few measures. As is often the case in deceptive cadences, the actual granting of the tonic pitch in the melody intensifies the disappointment, for we actually hear the note we seek, but misharmonized. (One can almost become aware of the E first, only then realizing the inaptness of the rest of the chord!)

As noted, however, we now have the period of E's "composing out" to rectify this harmonic wrong turn. But things only get worse: if the C^7 sonority that follows is intended as Italian sixth, it, like earlier directed types in the piece, fails to resolve, although iv approaches a i_4^6 (end of m. 22) that could serve as a pre-cadence item that the Italian sixth would point to. But this i_4^6 just slips back into augmented sixth—the dead end in m. 23, all the more crabbed in its diminished-third "inversion" (not rare in Chopin's music: we will even meet another in Prelude No. 22).

The weighty silence reinforces the forlorn aspects of this lack of energy in the cadential drive (emotionally related to the lack of resolving force in the dependent-type chords along the way, as well as to the general falling trends in the piece). But the little coda, as it settles the melodic quest, sets to rights the harmony as well. The first chord can be understood perhaps as i_4^6, perhaps as V (both normal consequents to the pre-silence German sixth, and not really distinct harmonic entities in most cases anyway): if i_4^6, the F♯ anticipates V; if V, the E's, suspended across the silence, resolve, appoggiatura-style, to the D♯'s. Richer is to consider the chord a blend of tonic and dominant elements; for these now get disentangled and distributed into the two pure, untroubled chords that follow. The low E at the bottom relates to and outdoes the low B at the climax of m. 17, and generously supplies the root so provocatively missing at the start of the piece. The ongoing eighth-note motion has given way to the calm declaration of even half-note cadential pronouncement, and rest. The whole is a remarkable creation.

NOTES

1. A numeral under a carat denotes a scale degree.

2. The D♮ is not an "alternate" third of the B chord (which would remind us of the G♯ vs. G issue), but an appoggiatura to the C. The ending C–B segment echoes and balances the earlier, lower C–B on the other end of the treble V chord. The D is stuck onto the later C–B, and the D♯ and D in this measure simply behave according to normal seventh-degree usage

in the minor mode, the D♯ raised to resolve to E (downbeat of m. 13, embedded in the resolution of V to i), the D retaining normal (lowered) status to resolve down.

3. Of course these two processes are harnessed, forming together the indissoluble fabric of the music. The $\hat{2}$ at the end of part one is harmonized *in* the V^7 that the harmony has brought by that point, and so forth. For convenience only, the two dimensions are being considered separately.

Prelude No. 5 in D Major

A continual mixing of the modes pervades this brief piece, making ambiguous its emotional slant. Tiny details blend the openness of major with the darker, more closed seriousness of minor. This confusion is immediately presented in the opening dominant-seventh complex, in which an A dominant seventh is arpeggiated for four bars, with A, fifth degree in the key of D, embellished alternately by B, the normal $\hat{6}$, and B♭, the lowered or borrowed $\hat{6}$ (or, that is, the normal $\hat{6}$ in d minor). The even juggling of these neighbors (A–B–A vs. A–B♭–A) trades the mode and mood back and forth (and the alternation itself is called to our notice by virtue of the solo B–A introduction in the first two attacks—which may thus tend to sound like anacrusis).

The listening experience that follows is intense and difficult, due to the extremely rapid harmonic turnover (after the opening stasis, the chords change as often as three times per quick measure), the frequent wholesale transposition of small segments of music (making the key jump quickly and spontaneously in sequence from place to place), the absence of overt punctuating moments in the thick texture, and—thoroughly unlike any of the earlier preludes—no sense of a melody that is slower than, clearer than, truly distinct from the total detailed unfolding of the involuted surface tissue. (Consider in contrast No. 3, which features an equally run-on surface—with, however, a very slow selection of tones lifted out and strung along, above, as melody; and an underlying harmony that is extremely simple.)

Odd points of sudden stasis, however, are encountered along the way, and serve as focal points (which also echo the opening). In mm. 13–16 the music stops with a one-measure figure that is trapped and repeated. The opening and closing notes in this figure, along with the succession along the top notes, suggest an F♯ chord. (Actually, the figure is complex, but amounts to F♯: we can hear, by eighth-note beats, I–ii°–V in F♯, with the high A♯ as indirect anticipation of each next returning F♯ chord.)[1] But notice a curious detail: at the very end of this momentary obsession, the A♯ is replaced by A, a change in mode similar to that at the outset.

In m. 17 the piece starts over (first F♯ is settled on the downbeat, concluding the previous episode), and so we have another "catch" on A. Then we stabilize one more time, in two successive four-bar stretches of repetition, mm. 29–32 and 33–36, these squarely on D.

Thus, the rocks we use to step on solidly in crossing this turbulent stream are precisely chords of D, F♯, and A, the notes of the underlying triad writ large. In this scheme we find the F♯ inappropriately presented as III, which at the last moment reduces to iii; the A♯ that causes the effect reconstitutes and reinterprets the B♭ that was involved in a related modal moment in mm. 1–4. And it is confirmative that the final stasis on D is twice as long as the others, and uses figures that resemble the others (mm. 29–32 echo the F♯ business, while mm. 33–36 behave like the figure associated with A). Furthermore, the D area is modally mixed, and the note that single-handedly produces this effect is once again B♭ (as bass neighbor in mm. 29–32, as incomplete upper neighbor in the treble of mm. 33–36). Curiously, B♭ has the last word (as against the normal B, and unlike mm. 1–4): it stands uncorrected at the end, leaving a faint taste of minor into the otherwise major-mode cadence.

The active material that swirls between these points takes the form of single-measure clumps that basically state three harmonies each, all geared toward the chord on the following downbeat, which thus organizes or "grounds" the previous sounds. Motivically, a pattern emerges of upper-voice skips culminating in a downward step that echoes the B–A and B♭–A pairs from the beginning. (See Chopin's special beaming in those opening measures.)

All of it is studded with details designed to confuse the modes. In m. 5, just as the music gets going, A♯—that same pitch!—is used minutely as a chromatic passing tone. This introduces a chromaticism that is a frequent feature throughout, having its seeds in the initial chromatic detail of m. 2, and contriving to produce much of the moment-to-moment sense of modal ambiguity. If we severely slow down the motion of m. 5, which gives us I–IV–V^7 in D, we can hear the IV first as (borrowed) iv—due to the presence of the A♯—and then as IV (the A♯ giving way to the B). In the ensuing sequential transpositions Chopin seems to emphasize (briefly tonicize) naturally minor chords (ii and vi) of D. If he hits a major chord, he compromises its major sound in the same way—see the I in m. 7, beat 2: it first sounds as d, then as D (with E♯ then F♯).[2] More pointedly, V at the beginning of m. 8 is directly changed to v (which is how it shows up in m. 9, where it locally functions as iv/ii—the measure going i–iv–V^7 in e). Certainly these chromaticisms are microscopic, but in sum they produce the surface we hear. They are applied beat after beat, and even in slow motion would keep us continually adjusting our impressions of what chords we were hearing.

Finally, the use of whole-measure diminished-seventh chords, occurring at strategic points, contributes to the sense of mixed modes (such chords being native only to minor scales). Measures 12 and 28 are both single-chord measures, both e♯$^{°7}$; both occur precisely before stretches of static harmony, and they each end segments that in the large correspond to each other (the restart in m. 17 goes as far as m. 28; thus mm. 17–28 repeat mm. 1–12). The diminished sevenths themselves, which slow down the harmony, are signalled by an immediately prior slackening of activity: m. 10 nearly repeats in m. 11, before the diminished seventh in m. 12 (and similarly for mm. 26–28). The earlier e♯$^{°7}$ is applied (as leading-tone approach chord) to the F♯ that settles in at m. 13. The same chord reappearing in m. 28 acts as common-tone diminished seventh to the long I that follows.

The abrupt end to the perpetual motion calls forth the succinct cadence, in which the by now familiar third over the tonic chord echoes the one spit out at the end of the sixteenths.

NOTES

1. Even at this minute level, the modes are mixed: the ii° is of the key of f♯ minor, mixing with the locally prevailing F♯ major.

2. Again, the E♯ is a chromatic passing tone. And the D chord is more likely understood as IV / V, the measure going A–D–E to land on and briefly tonicize A on the next downbeat.

Prelude No. 6 in B Minor

The obvious change in both texture and manner, with the leisurely, poignant melody in the bass and a clear accompanimental pattern in the treble, is very welcome, along with the simple succession of melodic units.

The expansive arpeggio gesture and its cello-like registration contribute to the ruminative air of the piece. The rising arpeggio motive gently backs down by step. This retreat is not so plain, as the C♯ in m. 1 may at first glance appear to be a neighbor between the two surrounding D's; but the rhythmic emphases—the C♯ long and beat-stressed, as opposed to the short, weak D after it—make C♯ seem to move to the B, the next stressed note. Similar emphasis on the prior D leads us to follow that pitch through the C♯ and into the downbeat B: hence, the C♯ passes. This 3–2–1 motion at the top of the arpeggio is then clarified for us in immediate octave reduction at the end of m. 2 (into the downbeat of m. 3), and this clarification will reappear to end the melody altogether (mm. 23–24), where it will be more evident still, as the echo part will not be elided into a new arpeggio figure (as it is originally). It is useful to play this opening portion of the melody, stopping at the first note of m. 3, to convince oneself of the effect.

A very expressive aspect of the melody is the successive stretchings upon the original arpeggio. In m. 3 the melody starts out again (emanating directly from the tail of the step echo), but reaches up farther. (The 3–2–1 figure thus now comes out as 5–4–3, the two little step motions together filling out the entire b-minor triad.) In m. 5 the figure stretches even more, starting lower and ending higher, covering now a generous two full octaves. And finally the figure finds its grandest expression in m. 13, where it starts with the deepest pitch so far, and reaches broadly through two octaves and a third. This one brings a kind of satisfaction, as it is immediately repeated. Neither retreating nor advancing by steps, it halts the melodic motion for the first time.

These quietly dramatic motions can serve to carry us through the music by way of the harmonies they directly convey. The initial rise is of course on i, as is the second (expanded) one. Thus, with the 3–to–1 and 5–to–3 step motions, the entire first four bars are tonic harmony (contrasting nicely with the harmonic turnover in the previous two preludes). But the arpeggio of m. 5 suddenly flushes out the i with a lovely, broad VI, a substitution rather than any move onward or outward. This VI plays a crucial role in the life of the piece, for when the music starts up again after the important half-cadence in m. 8, the i once again gives way to the VI, but this time the arpeggio does not turn downward at the top, but continues to climb, by step, reaching an F (end of m. 11). With E as passing tone,[1] this pinnacle F finally inflects the G chord underneath as G^7, dominant of C; and so it acts, as C is ushered in, now to stay for a full three measures. It is this C chord, a large-scale Neapolitan in b, that is represented by the maximum expanse of the arpeggio figure. (But it is first sounded in $\frac{6}{3}$—the standard form of N.) Chopin is rather fond of root-positioned and tonicized N, and here it plays a central role in the composition, placed just midway in the music and almost rivalling the opening tonic in terms of duration. It is a moment of luxurious repose.[2]

The arpeggio form returns just once more, at the end of the piece, once again within a long tonic stasis, which in the large seems to balance the opening i. Together, they can make of the medial N a kind of harmonic neighbor. In fact, the low C in m. 13, the deepest sound so far, nicely gives way to the lower B in m. 22. One can learn to sense this (cadential) B distantly resolving the big, central C.

We can continue with the harmonic life of the piece by returning to the original VI in m. 5, whose local function is to lead from the opening tonic to the formal half-cadence of m. 8, by way of a sudden burst of chromatic energy and twisting. Curiously, at first the bold VI seems destined merely to subside back into i (last beat, m. 5), but then chords aiming at V appear (ii$^{\varnothing7}$/V, V$_5^6$/V for beats 1 and 2 of m. 6), leading to a long and complex dominant expression (starting with the vii$^{\circ7}$ of m. 6, beat 3). Significantly, some of these dominant items unobtrusively resolve not to i (b) but VI (G)—see carefully the last eighth of m. 6, and the second eighth of m. 7. Two diminished sevenths in a row (the first as vii$^{\circ7}$, coming directly out of i; and the second as vii$^{\circ7}$/V, going into V by way of i$_4^6$) lead into the half-cadence itself, marked by a settling upon root-position V, and a halting of the treble motion. But by this point we will also have noticed that the highest part of the treble has blossomed into melody, having emerged surreptitiously from the earlier repeated eighth notes that give the accompaniment its touch of life.

The change-over into restart is delightfully crafted. In imitation of the approach to m. 3, the bass steps down into the resumption. But at the same time, the two solo notes, D–C♯, make a more immediate echo of the final two melody notes in the treble. Our attention, having been gradually shifted to the top, is neatly brought back down by this imitative transfer. So the melody of the first eight bars has concluded on a pair of notes that, in resounding below, can extend into a three-note figure that refers right back to the beginning of the piece, which it now reintroduces. The earlier pairing of 3–2–1 figures was embedded in tonic harmony, with the C♯ as dissonant tone. This situation curiously reverses now, as the undisplaced harmony is the V, which recasts the figure so that a dissonant D absorbs into a harmonized C♯. The network of echoes, transfers and reinterpretations at this juncture is uncannily rich.

Later emerging from N in m. 14, we find ourselves effortlessly back into basic harmony, for with the slightest adjustment in the treble, N (C) turns into iv (e). We then seem to embark on a new melody for this second half of the piece. But it is not new; it is just quoted from the melody that emerged in the treble in m. 7.

This area harmonically features various forms of dominants of b, and a careful view of their resolutions again reveals the trading of VI for i on occasion. But there is one stunning instance of this that becomes in fact the point of the passage. At the end of m. 17 we have a very secure V^7, lasting two beats and strongly suggesting a solid tonic resolution to come. But in m. 18 we are disappointed. One can view beat 1 there as vii^{o7} (substituting for and thus prolonging the V^7), which then resolves not to i, but to VI again (beat 2). More effective, however, is to be persuaded by the strong downbeat bass G, signalling immediately the VI (with the treble tones simply suspending en masse from the previous measure): a full deceptive resolution matching the force of the V before it. The notable history of the submediant in this piece thus continues.

Deceptive resolutions of course require a reformulation of the V which can then resolve all the more rewardingly into i—and just this happens now. The prior phrase is repeated, and the V^7 in m. 21 this time fires correctly. The i of m. 22, with its deepest bass B, is indeed deeply satisfying, and forms the cadence of the piece; the rest is coda, and tonic.

A curious detail appears early in the coda, that strange A in m. 22, all the odder for the touch of prominence Chopin bothers to give it with the accent. It renders of the i a rather mournful minor seventh, but also seems to make a stab at passing downward (to the F♯, to which it stumbles rather than passes). If so, perhaps the earlier 3–1 and 5–3 connections are here joined by an 8–5, to complete a total tonic outline.

A few delicate touches follow. The last, reminiscent arpeggio starts out of a tied note, which lends it a sweetly tentative quality that helps to avoid any sense of energetic reprise here, which would fight against the peace found in resolution. (Try playing the passage by restriking the B at the beginning of m. 23: it sounds as if the piece were suddenly to start up again for more development.) Then the accompaniment ends in the treble on $\hat{5}$. That A in m. 22 has brought our top voice down from its accustomed position on B to the less firm position of the fifth, from which, after a disarming little hesitation, it flutters limply into silence.

NOTES

1. The E can variously be heard as anticipating the E on the next down-beat, or, for that matter, as blending with the treble to sound iv. In these cases, however, the F, as nonscalar neighbor, still blends with the mea-sure-long G chord to yield the G^7.

2. Such a stasis upon N is actually a familiar compositional habit throughout the common-practice eras, beginning with the Baroque. See, for example, the end of the piano solo that opens the second movement of Mozart's A-major Piano Concerto, K. 488, where we sit on the lowered II as if it were a comfortable, deep armchair from which it is difficult to rise.

Prelude No. 7 in A Major

It is perhaps because of its innocent simplicity that this little piece is so famous. In phrase, in form, in harmony, there is an unruffled regularity. But it is due to this very condition that the one point of departure, in m. 12, is so successful.

To grasp the significance of what happens in m. 12, it is first necessary to understand that the harmony prior to that changes every two bars. This is apparent visually in the bass, where two measures of V will readily be seen to alternate with two measures of I. But each chord enters in considerable distortion due to step displacements in the treble: the downbeats in the odd-numbered bars contain treble notes that are a step away from the true chord tones. Resolutions take place with the following sixteenth, and the fully realized chord is then stroked in reassuring repetition until it sits stably as the lengthened note of the next downbeat.

This distortion feature, itself a regularity, enriches the simplicity underneath. The exact analysis of these non–chord tones depends of course on their precise dispositions. Taking m. 3 as a model, we see the D♯ and B♯ as appoggiaturas to the E and C♯;

some, as in m. 7, are simple suspensions. Even these two instances reveal how the enrichment is sometimes chromatic, and the resulting temporary sonority a considerable delight (the squashed effect of diminished triad in m. 3, the rough major seventh in m. 7).

The underlying harmonies are always uninverted, with the deep bass tone leaving no doubt about what chord we are to expect when the wrinkle is ironed out (with the curious exception of m. 1, where the lone treble C♯ is consonant with the bass, almost suggesting tonic before V is clarified; the recurrence of this moment in m. 9 yields an inadvertent iii instead).

With these hitches, all otherwise proceeds smoothly, until in m. 12 the chord from m. 11, which we are thus led to expect will continue on for one more measure, changes. So there is a sudden disrupting in the harmonic rhythm; and the chord of this change is itself a departure, being neither tonic nor dominant, nor in fact in the key at all. What we passively expect here is simply I, but what we get is a chord that even denies the essence of I by containing an A♯. This climactic point is led up to by way of a crescendo, and forms the thickest sonority of the piece (thick enough to be trouble to play). At the same time, the unchanging melody note that still overrides the moment assures its perfect integration into the flow of the piece.

The chord is, of course, $F\sharp^7$, to be understood as V^7/ii, proceeding then to ii (downbeat of m. 13—again, the bass B defines the chord, with A♯ and C♯ suspended). This resolution after one measure just continues the quickened (doubled) pace of harmonic change, which then remains at this rate of one chord per bar until the last two bars, when tonic harmony is restored, and, with it, the original harmonic rhythm (the two bars for I also serving to emphasize and stabilize the arriving tonic). The climax chord thus seems to explode the complacent regularity of what has gone on before it; the motion then seems to parachute gently down, by cycle of fifths (the ii goes to V) into the tonic.

A second aspect of simplicity is the even split of the little piece into two parts, a full restart commencing with the pickup to m. 9. What is left undone at the conclusion of eight bars is signalled by the presence of the third degree, C♯, over the tonic chord.[1]

This third degree can alert us to a piece-long linear structure that joins with the harmonic and phrase plans already discovered.

The music starts out with a prominent third degree on the first downbeat (thrust handily at us by the pickup). That C♯ immediately gives way to a B, second degree (the D sixteenth note seeming only to escape in the wrong direction). This repeated and then settled B needs an A to resolve it. The melody from there seems to search for this sufficiently convincing 1̂, which would also complete a 3–2–1 descent from the opening C♯ (thus, a walk through the bottom interval of the basic sonority of the piece). In fact, the melody seems to avoid this A. It does make one weak appearance, in m. 7, where it is approached from the wrong side. The teasing A♯ in m. 5 is otherwise as low as the melody gets. The high A in mm. 3–4, a proper gestural answer to the B, is ineffectual for resolution, which must be by step.

The first half of the piece ends with C♯ still firmly in place. So the music starts out again, delivers the C♯ again into B, and, after again heading off into other regions, picks up with the B in m. 15, this time to deliver it decisively into A, finally fulfilling the quest set up at the very outset. What alerts us to this outcome is a telling change in the patterning of the melody: at each dotted-eighth–sixteenth moment, starting with the one in m. 1, the move is up by step. This final time, however, the step is down. It is, in fact, the crucial downward motion of 2̂ into 1̂, which, moreover, exactly coincides with the arrival of V into I after harmonic departure, and with the restoration of normal harmonic rhythm. The repeated high A at the end would seem thus to be a "descant" or overvoice, the true last pitch of melody being the sustained middle A, nicely introduced a shade early by the grace note.

A few curious moments along the way: in m. 5 a prominent ninth, F♯, is added to E[7]; this sonority recurs in m. 14 (here the F♯ seems left over from the prior b minor; in m. 5, however, it seems quite gratuitously added to the chord). And just prior to this second instance, an inner-voice passing tone (curiously, A, the tonic—just as the tonic has momentarily disappeared in favor of A♯) enlivens the otherwise static repetitions of this part of the pattern.

Finally, there is a notorious pedalling problem at the end. Throughout, the pedal needs to be changed on the second beat of those measures where the chord has been distorted on the downbeat; only then can one sustain just the pure, fully realized chordal sound for the remainder of the two-measure unit. Fortunately, the bass form is such that the recaptured sound is in most cases still in root position. (A big exception, mm. 7–8, is actually fortuitously useful: if one changes pedal on beat 2 to eliminate the downbeat suspended G♯ and D, one ends up sustaining not tonic $\frac{5}{3}$ but tonic $\frac{6}{4}$; but this instability plays well into the structural aspect of the moment, for it provides an additional motivation, at the end of this first half, for the second start to come.)

The difficulty at the end is that if one changes the pedal in m. 15 (again to clear the unwanted downbeat notes), one loses the deep A. True, one is not then left with the second-beat $\frac{6}{4}$, as in m. 7, because a further bass adjustment restores root position,[2] and one can change pedal yet again there to prevent the unwanted E from sounding through. But the remaining high bass A will not convince, in terms of other, deeper notes that have come before.

A solution in performance is to stretch the music slightly on the sixteenth at the end of beat 1, m. 15, so as to change the pedal just as the left-hand pinky is still holding the deep A. Thus that tone will be captured by the pedal to sound through to the end.

The occurrence of a third degree over tonic harmony halfway through the piece having been such a force in terms of overall form, phrase, and melody, this prelude naturally must not join some of the others in ending in imperfect form. The triple high A at the end, recalling that of m. 3, works with the deep A (echoing m. 7) to wrap this elegantly neat composition in a satisfying tonic package.

NOTES

1. And only incidentally by the presence of E in the bass; the chord is still in $\frac{5}{3}$, the deep A controlling the harmony in such "oom-pah" patterns. The E is, however, the last bass note struck, and will mildly destabilize the moment.

2. A necessary change in pattern even if the deep A can be retained: we do not want the final *struck* bass note to be other than the tonic.

Prelude No. 8 in F♯ Minor

A plunge into hectic and unremitting turbulence dispels the transparency of the prior music. The new, richly dense texture runs a breathless course unmarked by clear surface variance, and so the "story" is challenging to follow and assess. The observation of several simplifying factors is essential in approaching this intense composition.

First, the profuse surface is readily reducible to a melody with accompaniment, with the latter arpeggiating chords in a single shape. The highly embellished treble comprises both melody and elaborating figuration, as clearly indicated in the beams and stems. The upper part pits an even eight attacks against the bass sextuplet speed, which adds to the overall sense of clutter. But two of the six tones swirling around the melodic notes in repeated pattern are just upper-octave echoes of melody (on the model of the first prelude, which this piece recalls also in terms of melodic rhythm and shape); two others, notes five and six in each beat, are chord tones; and the remaining two, notes three and four, decorate the fifth tone in surrounding steps. These invariant features make more for complication than real complexity.

Second, in the long-range unfolding, landmarks do occur, by which we can orient ourselves. Certainly m. 2 repeats m. 1; and this immediate restart will be followed by two others, at m. 5 and m. 19. Sequences and near-sequences abound, and mm. 15–16 repeat in mm. 17 and 18 (except for the last beat of m. 18, which is changed to prepare for the restart at m. 19). A registral and dynamic climax is clearly felt at m. 22, after which the harmonic language and melodic motions both simplify greatly.

But if these considerations help to clarify a formidable surface, we find an inexorable complexity in the harmonic language. And as the surface changes beat by beat only insofar as the harmonies change, an intense technical appraisal of the chord succession is unavoidable in accounting for the piece's very strong effect.

The opening measure is simple enough: the four beats, distilled according to the ideas suggested above, present the progression i–i^6–$ii^{\varnothing 7}$–V^7.[1] As noted, m. 2 just repeats m. 1; but in mm. 3–4 our first difficulties appear. Dominant-seventh sonorities on different roots occur on beats 2 and 4 of m. 3 and on beats 1 and 4 of m. 4, and only the last one moves on to resolution (in the new beginning at m. 5). Such chords, of unclear functional intent, are in fact the essence of the harmonic style here, and a close examination of these two measures is a prerequisite for further like encounters down the road.

The entire two-bar area descends into the "true" V^7; but this fairly straight line is not composed of mere passing sonorities. Rather, the perfect sequential relationship of the two halves of m. 3 can help us grasp that the chords can be heard in pairs, with the first two beats, d$\sharp^{\varnothing 7}$–G$\sharp^7$, acting as $ii^{\varnothing 7}$–V^7 in c$\sharp$; the same progression then appears in b. Thus, the music *points* but *falls short of arriving at* two primary areas of f$\sharp$—its dominant and its subdominant.

But then m. 4 only superficially resembles its predecessor; its inner harmonic workings are quite different. Here it is the *first* chord of the first pair that is the dominant-seventh type (spelled as German sixth in some editions). This chord seems to function neither as a dominant seventh nor as a German sixth (the two usual roles of this sonority). Approaching the measure backwards, we find the beat 4 V^7 preceded by its associate, $vii^{\varnothing 7}$; beat 2 is the same chord spelled differently (perhaps influenced by beat 1). That leaves the first beat as a passing sonority that just lowers the $F\sharp^7$ before it, on its way to the functional harmonies of beats 2 through 4. These uses of the dominant-seventh sound will establish precedents for later occurrences.

The restart in m. 5 is more ambitious than the original. The evident climbing force of the melody, which had crested in m. 3, now intensifies: m. 6 does not just repeat m. 5, but starts it and then stretches it upward (ending on another nonresolving ii^7–V^7 pair, pointing at III). Consequently, m. 7 brings the music of m. 3 a third higher.

And at this point the appearance of nonstandard dominant-seventh chords intensifies as well: we have them now on beats 2, 3, and 4 of m. 7 and on beats 1, 2, and 4 of m. 8. (This includes five in a row!) Again they are subsumed under a long, downward slope, and again the melodic sequencing (in half-note units) suggests we consider the chords in pairs.

The first pair is another floating ii–V group, in E. The last pair, at the end of m. 8, is another: $ii^{\emptyset7}$–V^7 in C$\flat$. But the middle four chords are all perfectly parallel descending dominant sevenths. Still thinking in pairs, though, we can enrich the notion of mere passing chords by invoking the model of German sixth–to–V^7, which presents two dominant-seventh sonorities in half-step descent, the first resolving to the second. (Indeed, in some editions the spellings here support just this interpretation.) Throughout, however, we must note that these partial and various progressions do not just fail to reach resolution, but may point at places that have no significance in the original key of the piece.

The last dominant seventh in m. 8 will initiate a new region in the music, via a new type of connection. We are used to hearing the second chord in these pairs as a resolution, but this time this $G\flat^7$ will itself seem to resolve onward, being followed on the next downbeat by a $B\flat^6_4$, which is a correct goal of $G\flat^7$ in the key of B$\flat$ if the $G\flat^7$ is taken as a German sixth. By normal usage this $B\flat^6_4$ would then be a stabilizing force, suggesting a following F^7 and B$\flat$ cadencing.

With great effort we can now trace some B$\flat$ music, up to beat 2 of m. 11, where we do find a V^7–I pair in B$\flat$. The process that leads from the suggestive ("cadential") $^6_4$ to the two-place "cadence" here is more cumbersome to describe than to hear. An F pedal in mm. 9–10 underlies two beats of dominant applied to c (ii of B♭, end of m. 9 and the following beat), sequencing to the same treatment for d, iii in B♭ (last three beats of m. 10).

But is this key in any way pinned down by the emerging V^7–I? Absolutely no surface notice is taken of this harmonic event, and, in fact, we at once move to another key, the last two beats of m. 11 tonicizing g minor. Again with no chance to breathe we have E♭ tonicized for us (m. 12), and then C♭ (mm. 13–14). These keys have moved down by thirds (B♭–g–e♭–C♭), but it is otherwise hard to know what to make of them in terms of any larger functional status. This condition certainly contributes to the restless feeling of the piece.

E♭ minor is again the focus starting at m. 15: the alternation is between $f^{\varnothing 7}$ and B♭, the same two-place progression working as $ii^{\varnothing 7}$–V in e♭ minor. But just as we seem to stabilize here, with four bars of repeated progression and even repeated music, a very sudden shift occurs: the last beat of m. 18 takes the melodic F of the B♭ chord and treats it as the E♯ of a $C\sharp^7$, and at once the dominant of our basic key appears, succinctly introducing the reprise at m. 19. So we start off again without having settled anywhere else, and with little more than a voice-leading integration of those intermediating keys.

The final restart, consistent with the agitato and stretto direction found there, intensifies further the surging thrust of the piece. Measure 20 is already in the progressive form of m. 6 (not the tame repeating form of m. 2), but in m. 21 the last two beats of m. 20 are sequenced upward a step: and then in the last two beats they are pushed up yet another step—these moves bringing an urgency and sense of straining forward. And this last sequence is altered to reach even higher: beat 4 of m. 21 turns melodically up, keeping and inverting the chord won on beat 3, which it delivers into the fortissimo downbeat of the next measure, again inverted and again higher. These registral advances coupled with the trapped tension of the diminished-seventh chord gather the momentum of all that has gone before to deliver it into a grand German sixth, which itself is forged out of the diminished seventh (by just substituting D for D♯, m. 22, beat 3). On the downbeat of m. 23 this D-based German sixth resolves to a fundamental tonic $^6_4$ that is the grounding moment of the entire piece—and, of course, the point of climax. The climatic progression German sixth–i_4^6 in a sense justifies all the prior, and variously meaning, dominant-seventh sonorities that moved down by half step.

The decrescendo accompanies a precipitous fall (through chords readily analyzed in the home key) until the tonic $_4^6$ is restored in the lower register, downbeat of m. 25. Gradually over eight beats, with a G♯ bass passing tone (m. 25, beat 3) and a tantalizing suspended F♯ (m. 26, first two beats), this cadential $_4^6$ will find its way into V (last two beats of m. 26), and thence to a quiet i, downbeat of m. 27. The expanded cadential progression i_4^6–V–i has brought the music from the point of acute climax to a level of composure. The opening register of the piece is restored, but gone is the original intensity, for m. 27 is all flat repetition, the melody for four beats unable to rise into neighbor D (which keeps the whole embellishing figure down in place on C♯). Thus, this moment may recall the other restarts, but is cadential rather than progressive.

Peace has provisionally been found, but such has been the energy all along that there is much spillover now, and the coda that stretches from here to the end continues to rumble, if quietly. The harmonic and melodic behavior is vastly simplified. The melody seems intent on accomplishing the original theme, slowly finding its way to D and F♯ in inert remembrance of m. 1. Meanwhile, the bar of static i begins a slow plagal progression, the iv of m. 28 supporting the only remnant of the old up-reaching tendency. The return to tonic, curiously, is in the form of I, a modal mixture that flushes the surface with a hushed sweetness. The entire plagal area is now repeated in major, with IV in m. 30, as if in peaceful acceptance of the melodic impotence. The fallback into tonic is modally quirky: first it is major, completing the formula, but then it spontaneously reverts to minor (m. 32), a cancellation of the hope that has expanded modestly with the crescendo. Perhaps the tiny dynamic swell here is all that is left of the earlier energies.

A glowing III pops out of this long tonic, with the sudden cessation of all surface bother. The closing progression piously outlines the f♯-minor triad, going III–V–i, but N connects III and V, its lowered $\hat{2}$ continuing the deflating effect of I–turned–i. The pure sound of the final tonic is delayed by the lazily suspended E♯

repeating in the i. (Chopin's notation is unclear here.) Certainly the storm began moving out directly after its most intense moment; but even so, the dead pose in the last two bars forms an unexpectedly sobering conclusion.

NOTE

1. Again as in the first prelude, two melody tones interact with the chord in each beat. As these two are so often a step apart, usually there is no doubt as to which one is chordal. In beat 1 of m. 1, the D is a neighbor; in beat 4, the order is opposite, with the A appoggiatura to the G♯. But ambiguity arises in beat 3: F♯ blends with the bass to yield the $ii^{\varnothing 7}$; but E♯ makes it rather $vii^{\circ 7}$. Both chords make sense in the progression of the measure, and one can just as well hear $ii^{\varnothing 7}$ *becoming* $vii^{\circ 7}$. These two chords, three-fourths identical in content, are thus not fully distinct harmonic items in this context. (See m. 5 of the first prelude for a similar situation.)

Prelude No. 9 in E Major

Uniquely, this piece takes as its starting point a moment from an earlier prelude: the first three beats here are a quotation from Prelude No. 2 (m. 21). Otherwise, the music presents a singular mood, a crashing *maestoso* in an unrelieved, deep registration and thick texture. Different also are certain curiosities of line and chord.

First, however, is an oddity of rhythm: the constant accompanimental subdivision is in triplets, but in the registrally surrounding melody and bass lines the slow, quarter-note motion is enlivened by pre-beat sixteenths and thirty-seconds. Now, it is not really clear that the composer wants the triple-duple distinctions honored. Taking beat 2 of m. 1 as a first case, we may wonder if this is notationally part of a long tradition—certainly familiar in Bach, for example—in which the flagged B would be meant to coincide with the third triplet-eighth; given the complications inherent in compound meter notation, the dots and flags that seem to introduce duple subdivisions are often mere conveniences.

But by beat 4 we realize that at least the distinctions between the sixteenths and the thirty-seconds must be intentional. The situation may still adhere to the tradition of convenience, with the sixteenths meant as third triplet-eighths and the thirty-seconds as pickups twice that fast (the last sextuplet-sixteenth of the beat). In any case, the distinction here seems oddly applied. At first the melody makes use of the slower (sixteenth) type of pickup while the bass line (itself rather melodic, especially in mm. 3–4, where it gets unusually fussy) uses the quicker one. But later the bass type takes over in the melody (but for a curious exception in m. 10).

Also, at first these figures do not disturb each other. In mm. 1 and 2 they occur separately, and, if performed accurately, may seem rather capricious, perhaps "interpretive," in effect. But in m. 3 they directly collide at the end of beat 2, and if all along one has been scrupulously maintaining the difference between these figures and the triplets, then at this moment we approach beat 3 with three distinct pickup time points all jumbled at the end of beat 2!

This combining continues, with joint appearances in m. 4 (beat 2), 5 (beat 4), and so forth. Perhaps then we must take as a special signal the lone case—m. 11, beat 4—where the two figures coincide as the same type: for this one is pickup to the final downbeat of the music, aimed at the tonic chord that resolves not only the immediately prior (and difficultly won) dominant but the piece itself. All in all, the music seems more quirkily interesting if the notation is taken at least somewhat literally.

For most of the composition, a rich harmonic life matches the thick texture. No hint of complexity is heard at first, however, as an initial four-bar phrase moves through strictly diatonic harmony (pure triads at first, soon clouded by added sevenths) until an applied dominant (m. 4, beat 2) leads to a concluding V and then a new start. This much of the harmony has supported a slow but very simple melodic climb from B up to E and back again— that is, along the E scale through an interval of the E triad.

But in m. 5, as this music begins to repeat, strange distortions, both melodic and harmonic, begin to appear. What had originally been the purest I–V–I (m. 1) is now suddenly I–V–♭III, with the G-major triad of beat 3, m. 5, supplying a delightfully surprising substitution, not just of mediant for expected tonic, but of borrowed mediant, which introduces two foreign pitches at once. There were slight chromaticisms in mm. 3–4 in the V/V and the bass neighbor tones, but suddenly here the chromaticism is intensely felt. This surprise chord not only leads immediately to further-reaching chromaticism in that it is directly applied as dominant for the C chord that follows, but serves as the model for the chromatic features through the remainder of the piece, which are of the mode change and quality change sort.

At the same time, melodic peculiarity is begun. For with this repeat the interval B–to–E is once again walked through, slowly, in the melody, but the connecting steps are now C and D, the tones of the parallel (e-minor) scale. So a mixing of the modes in the harmony is coupled with a similar treatment of melody. But, furthermore, the C and D are themselves not even the usual *ascending* passing tones in e minor, and so the odd modality of the passage is emphasized. If we play an outline of the melody by itself in even quarter notes, eliminating all repetitions at each step, the modal switch in the second climb will be most striking; but when the harmonies are added and the process is slowed down and expanded the effect may seem somewhat blunted.

The E scales and tonic chord supply the route and goals of the rest of the melody. The climb to E that starts in m. 5 is accomplished faster than the original one, and the beginning and end points (B, E) are marked by repetition. But this time the E is just a way station, for, after lingering on it, we climb further by step, as high as G♯ (m. 8, downbeat), third of the E chord (and here spelled as A♭). Again, the connecting steps, F and G, are not the proper ones of E (nor even of e, with that lowered second degree). The G♯/A♭ is the climax, the height of the long crescendo and the point of maximal registral spread. From here, both these features contract.

The melody's only jump brings us down off the height, and we wander back to B, where we again linger, and then slowly climb up one last time, again to E. This last ascent begins with one more restart of the piece. The climb is also along the uncorrected e-minor scale, but at the last moment the lowered $\hat{7}$ does move through raised $\hat{7}$ to find its way into $\hat{8}$.

This slow and awkward-stepping stroll through the intervals of the E triad continues to be harmonized in aberrant ways that grow out of the surprise G chord in m. 5. The C chord of m. 6 that results from the G^7 extends the modal mixture, as borrowed VI. C too turns into a dominant, to suggest going further afield; but a surprise appearance of A major leads soon to a cadencing on A♭, which is strongly signalled by the climactic $A\flat^6_4$ in m. 8. The link from A to A♭ is the diminished-seventh chord on beat 2 of m. 7. It grows out of the A by double common tone; a passing chord on beat 3 leads to the same diminished seventh on beat 4, now spelled so as to resolve to A♭.

The bass of the $A\flat^6_4$ is the bottom of a long, slow stepwise descent that starts with the G of m. 5. Coupled with the rising step motion of the melody, this helps smooth over the appearance of odd chords, which thus emerge by very convincing voice leading.

The $^6_4$ surely fires correctly, moving promptly to $E\flat^7$ and thence to $A\flat^5_3$. As was suggested in terms of the melody, this A♭ must be a convenient spelling of G♯, the $\hat{3}$ of E, and thus a sensible place for the harmony, like the melody, to aim for in the center of the piece. In fact, the spelling is corrected at the end of the measure, where the chord is also adjusted to minor, the normal iii, for a iii–V–I arrival into the new start in m. 9. The climactic form of the mediant harmony, as major, seems especially expressive of the pride and grandeur in the prelude; it is also a prime instance of the modal confusion (or in this case, more specifically, confusion of individual chord quality, a very similar effect).

The remaining harmony is further distorted from normal usage. What had originally been IV (m. 1, beat 4) now comes out as iv (borrowed harmony). But in short order this a-minor chord forms a pivotal link into a three-chord series in F, first three beats of m. 10; the borrowed iv is thus also iii in F. Then the whole business is sequenced up another step, into g. The B♭ chord of beat 4, m. 10, acts like the a of m. 9: first as IV in F but resolving as III in g. The g area switches mode as its tonic–dominant–tonic pattern ends, with the sudden G major on beat 3.[1]

Since we go directly into cadence now, with V–I, we must hear this g/G as a kind of mediant in E, so that the progression since restart has gone E (m. 9)–F (m. 10)–g/G (m. 11)–B–E. The E triad is outlined, with F as passing area (thus *not* as Neapolitan), but, as with so much else in this piece, the mode, steps, and qualities are irregular. The F area is built on the wrong second degree of E, and the G area is correct as mediant only for e minor (with, additionally, the g-minor form of it wrong at that).

The kind of distorting mirror this piece seems to hold up to the world of E can perhaps be summed up according to the jumble of mediants found in it: we have the normal g♯ minor, the quality-enhanced G♯ major (as A♭), the borrowed G major and the quality-depressed / borrowed g minor! These mediants together explore a widened, emotionally enriched E, in the sense that the mediant chord expresses the middle note of the tonic sonority, the note that controls the key's modal status, its basic emotional state.

NOTE

1. The whole passage proceeds by transpositional quotation of the first three beats of the theme.

Prelude No. 10 in C♯ Minor

One of the most satisfying successions in the preludes is achieved by the skittishness of this piece in contrast with the weight of the prior one; and, running its course in only about twenty seconds, this is certainly among the most succinct statements in the group.

So tiny a piece has only two kinds of utterances to make, found joined in a phrase of four bars as the descending cascade plus the slower-motion roundup. Form is produced by repetition of this two-part unit, first at the same key level (minus the pickup that triggers the first tumble, and with an alteration at the end), and then in the key of iv (f♯ minor), and one concluding time back in the tonic (with a little tack-on at the end). Thus, the four-phrase piece has a clear plagal transposition structure. But this less-than-usual plan is nicely understood as an augmentation of the harmonic essence of the phrase itself, which is likewise plagal.[1]

Indeed, the alternating sequence of chords that makes up the body of the little piece is of i's and iv's, c♯ minor and f♯ minor. The cascade above, of ornamental rather than melodic interest, throws the crisp chord alternation into relief. The alternation culminates in a slow half-cadence, with V gradually turning into V^7. Curiously, at the end of this figure, the addition of E to the top of a V that is otherwise all root makes of the final sound of V the equivalent of a i_4^6—which is heard surely as a V with E anticipating the return to i. The accent on the E is especially curious. (A transfer of hands makes the E directly anticipatory, actually.)

There is a minute change in the immediate repeat: A, the last pitch of the rapid treble notes, comes out now as A♯ (last attack of m. 6). The discrete difference helps introduce a more formal statement of v in mm. 7–8, which differ from mm. 3–4 in that they offer a full cadence in v. For now the scale arrives into G♯, downbeat of m. 7, by way of a 3–2–1 minor-scale bottom, and the G♯ can sound like a tonic.[2] (Play B–A–G♯ and then B–A♯–G♯ to verify the tonicizing tendency of the latter pattern.) We then have the full cadential formula on G♯, complete with cadential local-tonic $_4^6$, applied dominant, and final "i." In the g♯ chord of m. 8 the passing tones are from the g♯ scale.

Now the key of iv takes over: and thus the "alternate" chord of the basic phrase becomes the principal chord of the alternate phrase. The treble cascade begins not on $\hat{8}$ but on $\hat{5}$, which has the effect of rendering the new key less certain than the old. (Try the passage with a literal transposition of m. 1 for m. 9 to hear the difference.) At the same time, this change preserves C♯ as the top note of the descent.

The tag of this third phrase is twisted so as to restore V of c♯, preparing for the fourth phrase back in the tonic. The same accented anticipatory E occurs, as in m. 4. The fourth phrase then proceeds normally, and its tag is changed to supply, for the first time, a full cadence on i (mm. 15–16). But a strange surprise comes on the third beat of m. 16 in the form of an odd gesture: the tonic chord having finally been achieved in cadence, a texturally puzzling lone A, octave-doubled and even accented, is proposed and sustained in syncopation across the bar line. The hesitation is but momentary, for the composer seems to chuck it away with a shrug, repeating the cadence once more.

Technically the A is a kind of protruding neighbor to G♯'s. At least in the lower octave, G♯'s surround the A. (Note how the lower A actually sustains until the final G♯^{7} enters.) The upper A, though, sits well above its surroundings, more a step out of a "G♯

idea" in the chords on either side of it. But as a gesture this curious note, held out as if at arm's length for us to examine, may be heard to invoke the entire previous subdominant region (of which it is a prime tone). We can experiment with this notion by actually harmonizing this A with an f#-minor chord at this point; the flavor of the middle phrase will be captured. At the same time, the third-beat accented form corresponds exactly to the end points of all the earlier phrases (see beat 3 of mm. 4, 8, and 12). It is thus almost as if a fifth phrase might start on the next downbeat; instead, nothing sounds there.

The very last moment cutely isolates the last two chords by the tiny rest; and the E on top of V is still there in indirect anticipation.

The piece is neat, to the point, and, but for that A, very sure of itself. The moment at A, a charming glance backwards, seems a musical equivalent of "but wait a minute"—which is then followed by an "Oh, never mind!"

NOTES

1. A similar plan is found in the second of Gershwin's three piano preludes, where a first-section theme with a heavy plagal emphasis is followed by a middle section in the subdominant key. In both pieces a i–iv–i local progression thus expands into a i–iv–i modulatory plan.

2. The effect is definitively more successful than the similar slight alteration found in m. 22 of the G-major prelude.

Prelude No. 11 in B Major

A good way to approach this sunny and graceful little piece is to consider the lone F♯ thrust at us at the outset, and the similarly long B (m. 25) that marks the end of the melody. (The last two bars are coda.) The piece spends much of its time drawing our attention to a descent from the one note to the other, the $\hat{5}$ to the $\hat{1}$ of the key. The few other long notes along the way (mm. 13, 14, 21, and 23), all pitches of the tonic triad, stand sentinel as this trip progresses, falters, returns to start, and so forth.

But in order to follow this path it is necessary to understand something about the basic *contrapuntal* nature of the upper line. In m. 3 the succession of highest notes runs C♯ F♯ A♯ G♯ F♯ F♯ D♯. But it is useful to think of these notes this way: C♯ (F♯ A♯ G♯ F♯ F♯) D♯. The material in parentheses can be considered a separate, registrally partitioned strand of melody, woven together with the higher two notes to form a single surface succession. The stepwise connections *within* the registral regions help project this separation.

What we win by this view can be appreciated if we back up to the beginning. Everything about the opening moment promotes the view of F♯ as a note that is going somewhere. It is gently but firmly offered to us, with nothing to distract our attention from it. (The accent found on it in many editions is clearly expressive in this regard.) Then it is elaborated by neighbors on both sides, and, with the decrescendo, it starts to descend, all of this still solo. It reaches the C♯ as the body of the piece begins. Thus we have a $\hat{2}$ that is seeking a $\hat{1}$, and it is supported by a V^7 that obviously is tending toward its I.

Then, with the idea of the melody splitting at this point, we find ourselves snagged on this second degree, while the second-to-fifth eighth notes echo the opening neighboring of F♯. At the end of the measure the true line is reengaged, backing up to $\hat{3}$ and landing on the downbeat $\hat{2}$. It is the need to resolve this "stuck" $\hat{2}$ that becomes our story.

After a second interruption in the lower register, the $\hat{3}$–$\hat{2}$ is once again repeated, into the downbeat of m. 5, at which time a I chord arrives, and the $\hat{2}$, with its V, casually slips into $\hat{1}$. But with the line having been held up at $\hat{2}$ since the downbeat of m. 3, and with the accumulation of energy from the repeated attempts at moving on by backing up one step and pushing forward again, this resolution seems weak and insufficient, as if the energy passes on right through it.

What happens, then, is a repeat of the entire situation. The dynamic swells to restore $\hat{5}$, represented by the elaboration portion of the opening solo as found in m. 6, where it is supplied with tonic harmony accompaniment. And the result is the same: we get as far as $\hat{2}$, become stuck there, and weakly fall into $\hat{1}$ in m. 9.

One more time we restore $\hat{5}$ (downbeat of m. 10, again with dynamic increase), but for a little while now we depart from our basic story; in fact, the music moves *up* from $\hat{5}$.

All harmonies so far have been I or V; in m. 11, in this departure, we settle on a new chord, vi, introduced at the end of m. 10 by way of its own leading-tone diminished seventh. (This prominent vi—which will return again briefly tonicized near the end of the piece—may serve to introduce the key of the next prelude.) The melody meanwhile retains its split form (explicitly, by m. 13).

After some further harmonic exploration of the key, return to tonic harmony, at m. 14, comes in time to support the pronounced third degree, D♯, that mediates between the opening F♯ and the ultimately cadencing B of m. 25. This $\hat{3}$ gives way to $\hat{2}$ in m. 15, for a restart of the piece, and a reengagement of the basic line. Rather than backing up to $\hat{5}$, the attempt is braced at the point of issue, the second degree that has been trying to find its way home. The resumption eliminates the opening solo, to get right back to work.

Again, the opening phrase occurs twice. To introduce the second in this pair, the original solo line, m. 18, is harmonized even more fully than in m. 6. (Thus it becomes richer each time.) This last attempt, however, is abandoned prematurely: in m. 20 it seems to dawn on the composer that he hasn't been going about it right. So he backs up to a proper $\hat{5}$ again, m. 21—a true regathering of forces, for one last try. The fifth degree is roundly presented over I, and leads right into the original elaboration and descent. We get as far as the next triad station, $\hat{3}$, and pause. We then turn around $\hat{3}$, in imitation of the $\hat{5}$, and continue down. An anticipatory $\hat{3}$–$\hat{2}$–$\hat{1}$ (D#–C#–B, m. 24) is harmonized by vi (the other chord that, like I, can harmonize a D#-to–B motion). Again, the vi is introduced by its own dominant.

The melodic $\hat{3}$–$\hat{2}$–$\hat{1}$ is immediately repeated, this time with the corrected pair of chords, V–I. By anticipation the B eighth note announces the downbeat B that follows,[1] supported by root-position I and in its own full, uncluttered measure: the piece-long quest is fulfilled. As a token of approval, a gentle stroking of tonic harmony is offered afterwards as coda; curiously, it melodically presents $\hat{5}$ and $\hat{3}$, not $\hat{1}$—turning the solidity of resolution back into the imperfect condition of so many of the prelude endings. At the same time the exposed $\hat{5}$ and $\hat{3}$ seem to echo the pronounced F# and D# of mm. 21 and 23, themselves regrouped from their prior appearances in mm. 1 and 14.

One last thought: the repeated 3–2–1 figure in m. 24 matches its changing harmony in an odd way. Of course the chords themselves make perfect sense in progression; and the first naturally harmonizes the D#-to–B figure, with the intervening C# as (dissonant) passing tone. But the second chord is in a sense forced upon the melody above. Colliding with it, it calls forth a full permutation of who's who among the three melodic tones: it harmonizes only the C#, with D# then as appoggiatura to it, and B as anticipation. In slow motion the contrast in the two harmonizations is a curiosity.

NOTE

1. $\hat{5}$, $\hat{3}$, and $\hat{1}$ are each emphasized in just this way along this decisive passage: see the melodic repetitions of these pitches across the bar lines into mm. 21, 23 and 25.

Prelude No. 12 in G♯ Minor

Clear signals provided by the formula "German sixth–tonic six-four–dominant seventh–tonic" in a succession of keys help us follow the large-scale harmonic moves in this vigorous and forceful composition. These formations are especially advantageous given the refusal of the busy surface to ease up at formally critical moments.

As has been often seen so far in these pieces, the opening harmonic progression is simple and direct, even to the point of starting with a four-bar expression of tonic, as long as we look beneath the frequently chromatic melodic complications—at first passing tones, and then neighbors and especially suspensions. Great energy is felt in the opening steady rising treble line (whose individual tones produce a wide variety of colorful vertical sonorities with the underlying g♯-minor tonic chord), and the wide leaps in the bass arpeggiations. i–V–i–iv–V rounds back to i in m. 9 to fulfill an establishing presentation of the world of the key, and the opening music starts out again. But suddenly a foreign chord appears, the e minor of m. 11, which is the gate to the harmonic explorations to come. Although smoothly introduced as a voice-leading outgrowth of the tonic chord (they share a tone, and the notes that differ do so only by half step), this chord, a kind of altered submediant, will puzzle in terms of function until we grasp where it is going. By double common-tone link it is replaced by the G-based German sixth of m. 12. Then with the emergence of a B^6_4 to resolve the German sixth, the harmonic picture aims straight toward clarification, due to the strong tonicizing power of the cadential $^6_4$. In mm. 13–16 we find even alternations of B^6_4 and $F\sharp^7$, with the tension released in resolution on B, m. 17. The whole process can be seen to have depended on that sudden e-minor chord, an interruption in the middle of what should have been four bars of g$\sharp$ (for the melody continues on in mm. 9–12 as it did in mm. 1–4); it can now be assessed as the borrowed subdominant in B. (To hear the subdominant value of the e, play slow block chords to summarize mm. 11–17: e–"G^7"–B^6_4–$F\sharp^7$–B.) Indeed, the B is now alternated with e minor in a modally mixed plagal expression (mm. 17–20).

This new key of B undergoes interesting expressive changes. The three-beat pattern of I's and iv's reduces to two beats, for hemiola effect; and the B major itself deflates to b minor. This launches a new thematic area in m. 21, which seems to function as a transitional region, for b minor (again plagally inflected) passes through a minor (m. 24, also plagally given, and introduced by its own applied dominant), into G (m. 28, again treated the same). That G is only the briefest goal, serving immediately to introduce C. The way this C keeps giving over to B^7 (end of each crescendo, mm. 29–32) shows that it is acting as VI in e, which duly arrives in momentary stability in m. 33. The larger status of this e—which has been a iv in B (or b) since its pivotal appearance in m. 11—is suddenly given a forceful twist: it produces its own large, energetic dominant, the B^7 of mm. 35–36, and this turns out to act as German sixth for the next modulation! (See how the A of B^7 is at last respelled as Gx, m. 36.) A thunderous resolution to d$\sharp^6_4$, m. 37, initiates another firm application of the cadential $^6_4$ formula: we have, by whole measures, d$\sharp^6_4$–A$\sharp^7$–d$\sharp^5_3$ (switching to D$\sharp$ on the downbeat of m. 40). Thus, e-minor chords have both times ushered in German sixths leading to cadential $^6_4$'s to bring us from the key of g$\sharp$ to that of B and now to D$\sharp$. We thus traverse in the large

the overall governing tonic triad, g♯. And in token of this completion, we reach our established D♯ only to hear it turned promptly
into a dominant seventh, which ushers back the true tonic, and,
with it, a third start of the piece. (The change of d♯ to D♯ is thus a
step toward the emergence of D♯^{7}.) Throughout, the motivic features have adhered closely to the shapes found in the original
theme area.

The recapitulation goes as far as the double quote of the opening measures. But the second in this pair of restarts, m. 49 and on,
lacks now the ambitious e-minor twist that launched the piece on
its long modulatory quest. Instead m. 51 is E, a normal VI (the F♯'s
of m. 50 pass the bass to it), slipping right back to a conservative i
at the end of the four-bar stretch. The behavior of the piece now
alters considerably, showing especially a depletion of all that
energy, which seems then to have been geared toward the large
outline of i that the key changes entail. Starting in m. 53, alternations of iv and i (iv^7, with the B a pedal tone throughout) eliminate
the accompaniment motion, and by m. 58 the lower music has
dropped out altogether, with the previously restless treble
reduced to a single alternating, stuttering pair (a distillation of the
by-twos form of the melody throughout).

The eighth-couples are transferred below, where they cutely
scamper down toward the soon-to-be-reconstituted bass. Meanwhile, two treble tones join them, turning the evaporated iv into a
suggestion of ii^7 (which will proceed into cadence, ii–V–i).

Cadence now takes place, with the V^7 of m. 64 arresting the
motion altogether. The melodic B there is an indirect anticipation
of the i that follows.

There now comes a handsome coda. The basic manner of the
piece is present, but lacking the energy and drive; all is fairly
quiet, and confirmative of key rather than exploratory and out-
reaching. One tiny trip, however, will be taken.

The basic unit of the coda is iv^7–V^7–i. This repeats in mm. 66–67,
with this difference: the concluding chord is a deceptive VI
(downbeat of m. 67). Several further diatonic chords complete the
restoration of i, where the eighth-note motion halts (downbeat of
m. 69). The entire situation is started up again, but this time the VI,
E (m. 71), leads to chords of A, g♯$^{\circ(6)}$ and A$^{(6)}$. These three chords
bring us fleetingly into the orbit of A, the Neapolitan region of g♯.

The E has thus doubled as VI (deceptive) in g$\sharp$ and as V for the N. The N in root position has been seen in these preludes before, and will occur again. This time, though, little fuss is made of it, the connecting vii$^{\circ 6}$/N performing a standard function of passing between a root position "tonic" and its first inversion; thus the momentarily stabilized N immediately converts to the more usual N^6, whereupon it fits precisely into g$\sharp$-minor language in the most usual way, proceeding directly into cadence by way of the cadential $^6_4$. The composer helps us notice this little diversion into A by the ritenuto, which, however, is probably not sufficient to allow us to absorb the concentrated richness of the harmonic changes.

Silence separates the foregoing from yet a further coda. Here the pairs of eighth notes are only residual, in repeated i$^6_4$–V–i statements. A slow melody superimposed strains to produce the tonic interval D$\sharp$–G$\sharp$, which will then be used to sharply punctuate the finish. This interval expands from its lower note in stages: the lone D$\sharp$ grows to two notes, then three, and finally the full falling form. Curiously, while the individual terms of this growth fall, the overall progress is to rise, since each little descent starts a note higher. Thus, E of m. 75, sounding first as a neighbor to the surrounding D$\sharp$'s, is gradually reaching upward toward and through F$\sharp$ into the goal G$\sharp$; at the same time it is being set up as a *descending* passing tone.

Overall, the passage effectively recalls the first moment of the piece, now sapped of all drive. The original opening pair of notes tries once again to push upward, only to succumb and fall back to the starting point.

Prelude No. 13 in F♯ Major

As we begin the second half of these preludes, we find for the first time a composition of sufficient scope to have a true "form." In m. 21 there are so many conjoined changes in outward manner that we feel we are hearing a new section; while in m. 29 all the features of the original music are restored. Thus, the piece unfolds an ABA format. What clearly asserts B is a new tempo, a new melody (and considerably new melodic style), a different accompanimental manner, a markedly changed texture and, at least superficially, a new key.

An immediately striking aspect of the A section is the very slow progress of its melody. Not only do the successive notes appear at some distance from each other (at least as measured by the much more active bass motion), but the notes don't move around very much—the first three are the same, the next two differ minimally, then the original three again, and so forth. The result is to deflect attention from the melody, and on to the more attractive bass formation, which may even seem at first to present itself as melody.

The bass creates interest at once by introducing a dissonant E♯ into the F♯ (tonic) chord. Furthermore, this E♯, which appears to arise spontaneously, does not immediately resolve, but is followed by another (and milder) dissonant tone, the G♯. Then the two of them together get absorbed into the triad, at the F♯, which is capable of resolving them both. (Thus they are incomplete neighbors to the F♯.)[1]

We have then a tonic chord first smudged and then cleared; and this becomes the pattern for chord making in the A section. Each time a harmony appears, it is given this shape, with the second and third eighth notes distorting the sonority until the remaining three tones bring the chord into smooth focus.

Like the melody it supports, this harmony is at first very timid. Repeated A♯ melody notes are accompanied by repeated tonic chords. The move into dominant seventh, second half of m. 2, breaks the spell; but the opening is restored at once. A touch of impatience pushes the repeat of the placid opening forward—the pickup and quintuplet, which twists the underlying tonic into a series of neighbor-studded distortions.[2]

In m. 5 the music starts out a third time, but finally with some meaningful growth: along the expressive crescendo, we find the melody not again static but rising (through the triad), and when it reaches a high point, m. 6, we have, in place of the expected third sounding of I, a substituting vi, a welcome flush of change from the restriction to I's and V's. This vi, a locally consequential point as well as a significant link to later events in the piece, is handsomely laid out in generous registral spread, the bass dropping down to open up the space just as the high treble point is reached. The local working of this vi is signalled by the following $^6_4$ chord, which functions as a cadential $^6_4$ in the key of V, initiating the succession C♯$^6_4$–G♯^{7}–C♯, corresponding to the formula I$^6_4$–V^7–I in the key of C♯. As the cadence completes, the melody stops for the first time. The expressively rich vi was thus a pivotal event, doubling as ii in C♯ (in approach of cadence). The luxuriant roll on the V^7/V ornaments the cadence moment, raising it out of its surroundings.

The little bass wandering that marks time until the music of the beginning starts up again takes the last four notes of the six-note pattern and sequences it down by step. Thus the first four notes of m. 8 form a group, and the next four. At that point the four-note unit reduces to two, since the next two notes echo the large falling interval just heard. The idea will be clear if one plays with pauses between the groupings; but the bass line is much more interesting in its rhythmically undifferentiated state, the pattern parts blending subtly together. Furthermore, the sequence effect brings with it harmonic movement. The V at the end of m. 7 will drop to IV over the next four notes (since the last three in the six-note groups arpeggiate the chords), to iii in the following four, and—with the dissonant major seventh suggesting the A♯ is suspended out of the iii—perhaps even to ii (the B and G♯). Thus the chords gently waft down from the V that ends the first phrase to the I of the resumption. (The downward major seventh just as these first eight bars end may remind us of the original upward major seventh, which is about to occur again.) Finally, the shortening of the six-note unit in the sequence will create metric contraction, beats of dotted-half notes reducing to half notes (and perhaps quarters, at the end); these successive shortenings deliver us right into the reprise.

As the theme starts out again, the A♯ grace note added to the original first chord will directly absorb the last pitch of the bass solo, the G♯. It will also deliver up an octave the series of three bass A♯'s that lend a foretaste of the theme. All then proceeds more or less in order, with a few improvised embellishments. (The triplet chords in m. 11 sound rather impatient, as if the thrice-repeated tonics and slow melodic progress need a new push.) But a crucial change is about to occur, in a subtle but decisive form. On the downbeat of m. 13 we expect, by the strongest prior conditioning, a simple tonic chord, for that point corresponds exactly to m. 5, the resolution of the V^7. Instead we get an F♯-based dominant seventh, the E quietly but firmly inflecting the otherwise normal F♯ sonority so that, far from describing the usual home-base sound, the moment points out in a new direction; the chord both resolves the V^7 and twists the piece toward IV.

True to form, this chord must persist through its repetitions, lasting a measure and a half; this required extension of a chord that normally calls for prompt resolution increases the (always gentle) tension; and to further the effect, it outlasts itself, continuing right through m. 14, and even beyond. In the second half of m. 14 the melodic C♯ stretches expressively up to D♯, a heavily emphasized neighbor that intensifies further the expectation of resolution.

That resolution occurs in a specially complex manner. On the downbeat of m. 15 the initial bass B alone lays out the resolving chord, a long-awaited IV—such is the persuasion of downbeat bass notes. Otherwise, the entirety of F#^{7} is suspended above and through this B; the treble literally repeats the top three notes of F#^{7}, while the bass pattern does not follow the usual complex for B, its own lead note, but rather suggests more of the F#^{7} (especially the A#–C# ending, in the normal arpeggiating position of the figure). What renders the resolution process even more intricate is that in such a case we expect now a clean IV on the second half of the bar, treble and bass pattern both in agreement with the lead B. But close attention reveals that we get instead g# minor, a ii substituting for the IV.[3]

We hold with this convolutedly found ii, as a clear V^7/ii–ii progression follows. We then move quickly home, the ii fitting easily onto a cadential pattern, V–I. The treble A#, m. 17, a slow, indirect anticipation, beckons warmly.

The A section ends with some confirmatory harmony, including (m. 18) the IV we never did get a few bars earlier. A second luxuriously slow indirect anticipation, beat 4 of m. 19, ushers in the concluding tonic, and the melody comes to rest.

The last breath of the A section breaks an important regularity: the second six bass eighth notes do not repeat the first six, as they should if the chord remains unchanged. Instead, the last pitch, in place of C#, is E#. This move departs also in that we are accustomed to the last three in each group as chord tones, while this E# conflicts with the present harmony.

One can hear much in this pitch. As it rubs the F# chord the wrong way, it brings to mind that very first moment of the piece, where an E# likewise irritates in an F# chord; in fact, these last two bass notes of the A section are actually the first two as well. But as well, this E# performs a signal role, forging single-handedly the link into the next section. It resolves down by step to the d#, root of the next chord. Its origin is, most locally, the F# of beat 4: thus, it is a passing tone that connects at some little distance the roots of this and the next harmonies. But that F# is just a continuation of the downbeat F# of the measure, so the E# more broadly connects the two downbeats. But *that* F#, the cadence root of the whole section, represents the tonic of the entire page of music, as born in the first bass pitch of the piece. So the E♯ can be thought of as bringing the first bass note of the A section down by step into the first bass note of the B section. And finally, although the key of the second section will prove to be a matter of some ambiguity, at first it probably sounds like a modulation to the relative minor, d♯. In this sense, then, the E♯ connects the tonics of the two key areas of the piece. No wonder a grand stretching out of the bass line seems appropriate in performance at this point!

As noted, our middle section brings changes on many fronts; but several features bind the new music to the old. The melody, previously presented in terms of a three-note block sonority, is now a single-sound succession; while the accompaniment has changed from a single line to a pulsing three-note cluster. So the texture has been preserved but inverted. And throughout, the constant eighth-note motion is present (though now at a new speed).

The vi that opens the section is registered so as to capture and proceed from the vi in m. 6; the echo is unmistakable once we tune awareness to the outer notes of both soundings of vi, especially as the registral spread in the original instance played so expressive a role in its own passage. That first departure from the initial stretch of primary chords thus sparks this harmonically departing section.

Expressive elements abound here. The large, falling leap that starts the new melody is markedly different from the crawling theme in part one. The descending passing motion at the top of the bass staff (second half of the measure) adds inner-voice nuance. (The C♯ there passes from an earlier D♯.) The melodic B♯ is luxuriantly suspended into the next bar, where it only tentatively resolves to the C♯ sixteenth note: the longer, mid-measure C♯ does the job better.

Meanwhile, the key is in doubt. If it is indeed d♯ minor, then why B♯ as a descending passing tone (m. 21)? That pitch seems more appropriate in terms of the chord and possible key of the next measure, C♯ (note the tonicizing G♯⁷). Indeed, the entire two-bar theme is next sequenced down a whole step; so if we were prepared to hear vi, the opening sound of the B section, as new tonic, we would be bound to transfer that feeling and status to c♯, which would, through sequencing, inherit the tonic mantle. Meanwhile, a marked change of feeling comes with the deflation of C♯ to c♯ as the sequence moves into its second term.

The two-bar theme and its transposition make up half of the B section. The second half, preoccupied with the sixteenth-note figure that is unique to B, is readily heard in F♯, and in retrospect we can understand the theme itself as starting on vi and moving to V. Its transposition, then, goes from v to IV (where things remain for a while). We can conclude that the original key has never been left, but that its interior harmonies have been emphasized—for the moment in avoidance of the tonic itself. If we regard mm. 21–22 as ii–V^7–I in C♯ (the presence of that B♯ as inner-voice passing tone still suggests the d♯ is more than vi in F♯), then mm. 23–24 have the same progression in B, and the change of C♯ to c♯ is entailed in the role of the latter as ii in B. The theme of this section, then, just explores the primary interiors of F♯ (V and IV); the remainder of the section reorients toward home.

The arrival to I at the end of the section comes in the form of a double pedal, F♯–C♯, m. 28 (some ii is still lingering over it). The precise simultaneity of F♯ and E♯, sixth bass eighth of the measure, introduces that same throb from the A section's first and last moments. Then the accompaniment unobtrusively abandons the chugging form of B for the familiar pattern of the A section. Perhaps some performers are tempted to start the new (slightly faster) tempo at this point; but the composer seems clearly to want the bass of the A section played at the speed of the B section, to form a more subtle connection back into A. The same bass is then played speeded up a moment later.

The returning A section is, as is so often the case in ternary form, only a portion of its original self. In fact, we pick up in it just at the point of greatest issue—where I comes out as V^7/IV. Indeed, the B section having concluded not on a preparatory V^7 but with I itself, a resumption from m. 1 would seem intolerably bland; nor are we now in the mood for the gradual unfolding, both melodically and harmonically, that the earliest measures would bring. Instead, we are set back down right in the thick of things.

All proceeds much as it had been, but now a lovely descant is added, a voice over the top melody. And what had been such a compromised resolution of the long V^7/IV, actually to ii, now works out more smoothly, the first half of m. 31 simply suspending F♯^{7} materials across the lone B pronouncement, the remainder of the measure indeed supplying the rest of the IV to complete and confirm that B. Meanwhile, in m. 34, what had been IV (see m. 18) is now ii. So ii and IV have actually traded places between the original A section and its reprise.

The V⁷/ii in m. 32 has a poignant, and not very common, middle-voice pedal tone in it, the B repeated from the previous B chord and persisting until it becomes once again consonant (with the g♯-minor chord that is next). And the anticipations that accrue over the final V chord, last half of m. 35, actually assemble a full tonic sonority in advance: by the last moment of the measure, F♯, A♯, and C♯ all sound together (and this is perhaps all we hear, given the need to release the pedal at several prior points in the bar). The effect picks up on and expands the use of indirect anticipations at the end of the original A section (and in m. 33).

The tonic chord is widely spread, and lasts a full measure (36). The bass line exactly repeats in the second half of the bar, omitting now the important change in its last note that was so crucial in m. 20.

The return of that last C♯ to the deep F♯ could well end the piece; but a coda of marvelous and subtle compositional ingenuity rounds out the whole. Suddenly the submediant chord is introduced, chugging along in the texture and display of the B section: indeed, it is the chord that introduced the B section, that principally identifies all that is associated with the changes that take place at m. 21. The notated ritenuto will tend to restore the speed of the B section. The inner-voice descent quotes m. 21 (with B♯ now a proper B). Finally, the little sixteenth-note figure, strictly a feature of B, clinches the sweet reminiscence of the middle section that this coda elegantly presents.

The vi slips back into I—at such an odd place: not on some important beat, or even *on* any beat, but merely, casually, on the "and" of 5. The entire coda is harmonically vi–I, normally a very weak and in any case nonstandard cadence formula, but here it precisely refers to the two generating moments of the piece, those that represent the two sections. Such a coda, a complexly significant compositional summary rather than a mere afterthought, is a model of what the device at its best can be.

NOTES

1. Alternatively, since the E♯ and G♯ form a pattern with the next two notes, we can consider if this sequence of rising thirds suggests a pair of resolutions, the E♯ to the F♯, the G♯ to the A♯. Indeed, were the rhythm different, one might be compelled to hear it that way. If for example we had

then the sequence aspect would be emphasized, and the resolutions distributed accordingly. On the other hand, such a rhythmicization as

leaves no doubt for the original analysis. It is more interesting, perhaps, that Chopin smooths over the rhythm in such a way that neither interpretation is forced upon us, and we are free to imagine either.

2. The V⁷ that follows at first sounds like iii (a♯ minor), until we hear the A♯, suspended out of I, resolve down by step, and the intended sonority, V, is realized (in elaboration of m. 2).

3. The ii thus forms a *deceptive* resolution of the F♯⁷ (g♯ being the vi in the key in which F♯ is the V). The first half of m. 15 can also be heard as Fx°⁷ (over the B pedal): see the treble plus the usual three last notes. This chord would then substitute for the F♯⁷, and apply itself to the g♯ as its leading-tone seventh. It thus smooths out the deceptive process.

Prelude No. 14 in E♭ Minor

The second prelude having been such a strange piece, it should be
no surprise to find another. But the present piece, if less enigmatic
in such respects as key, chord formation, and stability of utterance, is otherwise odder, more unsettling—to the point, nearly, of
being a less thoroughly composed composition than the others.
Occasionally, among the later preludes, we do find one apparently made with less thoughtful attention (especially, for some
reason, among the minor-mode pieces); and while the resulting
expressions may yet add to the overall catalog of ways and means
in these nearly synoptic pieces, one must wonder if a certain
amount of creative fatigue may have resulted from the self-
imposed obligation to write in all twenty-four keys.

The e♭-minor prelude barely bothers to set up a texture; what
there is amounts to a single succession, doubled at the octave. Of
course, like any complex tonal line, that succession may be understood as a confluence of several vocal strands: for example, we
may view the opening three pitches, all of the tonic triad, each as
initiating its own succession, in which case, for instance, beats 2

and 3 bring an upper neighbor to the top voice, beats 3 and 4 a lower neighbor to the bottom voice, and so forth. At the same time these strands will join to make chords in progression (largely beat by beat); thus the first measure outlines i–VI^6–vii$^{°7}$–V^6. In addition, the path along the highest notes may emerge as melody, depending on the slant of performance and also the angle at which we find ourselves listening.

Thus, harmony and melody are fully fused. Fused as well are any successive "parts" of the piece, for the rush of ongoing sound does not isolate any motivic or gestural units, but seems to comprise a single, breathless motion for the entire duration. But progressive coherence is indeed discoverable. Simplest is that the piece achieves that most basic of landmarks, the full restarting, in m. 11. This aligns with the achieved ff, which again tapers off by the end; so the rise and fall of dynamics found in many of the individual measures predicts a similar shape in the large. The same relation holds for contour; the slight arch that shapes the upper line in the first measure is realized over larger spans, including the whole piece.

Further coherence lies in the fact that very often the total form of a given measure will be the basis for other nearby measures. Again at the simplest, m. 2 just repeats m. 1; but mm. 5 and 6 repeat this initial pair up a fifth (with m. 6 varying m. 5 in some oddly minute details, which are all the more curious given the intense speed of the passage of the notes). Meanwhile, m. 3 starts out like the first two, and departs from there; it itself is more or less sequenced in m. 4, which starts on III. Thus, over the course of the first six bars we move in chunks of repetition, outgrowth, and transposition, to outline the tonic triad, the III-level measure mediating between the tonic "theme" and its dominant transposition.

Measure 7 has a slightly new shape, but is then approximately sequenced into mm. 8, 9, and 10. Then comes the restart in m. 11, with m. 12 differing from 11 in again curiously minor details, and m. 13, like m. 3, taking off from the same place, to grow upward.

If we follow these measure-long units along the line of their highest notes—the one or two high points in each triplet—we find each has managed a slight downturn on or by its last note. From m. 13 this trend changes: this measure rises and stays steady, and m. 14, which almost sequences it, climbs up through to its last note, straining as it does so. Then m. 15 exclusively falls, and m. 16 actually remains flat along its top notes. This area, which starts at the climax, thus leads to a simpler vein, and the remaining three measures continue a process of simplification. Measure 17 reduces the action further by repeating itself halfway through; m. 18 begins by just reversing this half-measure; and of course m. 19 is just the cadence note, the tonic.

Meanwhile, very peculiar details populate this overall strangeness. After the opening pair of measures, the harmonies lose direction, definition, and clarity. How we get from i to III, from III to v, is functionally obscure (though convincing in voice leading). Then the four central bars of sequence transposition (7–10), though fostering a surface sense of order, further disorient both in terms of internally unformed harmonic content and equally unclear transpositional intent; the imitating measures seem tossed at random onto their new levels, where each declares its own approximate version of the previous, functionally inscrutable formation. The continual dynamic swells and ebbs match the turbulence in this situation.

Some of the tiniest details are bizarre. Minor triads built on leading tones introduce the two most important harmonic midpoints—a minor for the b♭ of m. 5 and d for the e♭ of m. 11. But even these nonstandard leading-tone effects are frustratingly blunted by anticipation: see the D♭–F at the end of m. 4, and, worse, the B♭–G♭–B♭ at the end of m. 10. And finally at the end of m. 15, the E♭'s and G♭'s anticipate and strangely neutralize the arriving tonic of mm. 16–19. But then the weighty A♭'s in m. 16 *delay* any convincing tonic sound, which is realized as a $^6_4$ in the second half of the measure.

But no cadential $^6_4$, this: it merely converts into root position, and this is all we will get for our cadence—no leading-tone motion into the tonic pitch, no dominant to introduce the tonic chord, nothing to ratify or confirm the final sound apart from the stabilizing enforcement of the reductions in surface activity.

This final prolongation is an oddity in itself. A regularized melody has at last emerged at m. 17, due partially to the reduction to two registral positions per beat, one of them a constant tone. The conflict of the upper voice with the beat, which has been present but probably not noticeable all along, now becomes apparent.

Throughout, the constant down-up pattern has threatened to group the eighths in pairs, as opposed to the beats of threes that are reinforced by harmony. But now that the harmony has become static, the pairs take over. Furthermore, the clearly emergent melody starts on the second eighth of the measure. As a result, this and the following bar will sound in six-four meter, with the downbeat shifted forward one attack. But then there will be a short-fall, for we must accept the very last note as a downbeat, and so the penultimate bar will seem to be cut short by one attack!

This little bit of stable melody, meanwhile, climbs from $\hat{5}$ to $\flat\hat{7}$, over the $\hat{1}$ pedal. So our tonic sonority will apparently contain the D♭, in a minor-minor-seventh chord (its third left echoing prominently from m. 16). And so it remains: by the end this D♭ is untouched, unresolved, and colors the last impression of stability over the final E♭.

The long decrescendo proceeds throughout this last stretch, as if the stability itself were receding from us rather than asserting itself. By the end, the music seems to have dropped off a cliff.

Prelude No. 15 in D♭ Major

Of all the preludes, the fifteenth is perhaps the one most suitable for performance alone. It is by far the longest, and, with the most fully developed form of the group, is least likely to come across as a compositional "impulse" or "suggestion." At the same time, it happens to be the only one that has managed to acquire a subtitle or nickname, "Raindrop," in obvious reference to the gentle patter of the repeated A♭.

For all this, the piece is by no means the most profound, enjoyable, or interesting. Sweet it certainly is, and it sustains itself convincingly throughout. Its long, sinuous melody, so characteristic of Chopin in a certain mood,[1] develops sufficiently to give the A section its own internal ABA shape. The brooding middle section, a surprising turn of events that seems to reveal a dark underside of the main music, is a little repetitious, and somewhat gross in its expression.

One can learn much about the piece just by following the course of the A♭ ostinato (which is relieved or enlivened periodically by the neighboring rise to B♭ and back). As the opening pair of phrases (to m. 8) consists exclusively of I's and V's, to which the Ab is, of course, a common tone, the effect is not strictly speaking that of a pedal tone. And when, as in the immediately following measures, the harmony and even key begin to move on, the Ab, potentially nonharmonic, stops—although its presence is still felt in the offbeat single note that continues as a feature of the bass arpeggiations, and that happens very frequently to be Ab anyway. Sometimes, as in m. 12, it serves as constant backdrop for the accompaniment figure, and then it does actually act as a pedal tone. In m. 13 it reemerges for a moment in its original manner. Then, after resuming its role as the opening music returns to round out the A section, it is left starkly pronouncing itself at the end (m. 27), under the fading and unresolving V[7] harmony.

With the sectional switch to parallel minor, the Ab (now spelled as G♯, with the key in enharmonic form) takes on a more prominent role, sounding now more sinister than soothing. The neighbor element is no longer present, and in the resulting relentless assertion the figure becomes the agent of growth to a towering insistence. Along the way it strengthens into octaves, and is further boosted, to the climactic B, when the harmony emboldens (m. 40).

In m. 59 the upper-octave position of the doubling takes over, and this has the effect of softening considerably the strident quality of the repetition; indeed, the entire expression relaxes now. Chords of i and V continue to predominate, keeping the G♯ safely harmonic; but in m. 63 it almost becomes a true pedal tone, clashing with the f♯ iv chord; however, it gives way, suspension-style, and resolves to the chordal F♯—only to reappear at once as a passing tone up to the A. As the downbeat half note returns the G♯, the departure has the effect of a neighboring elaboration around the ostinato tone.

Resuming its usual pitch value, it simultaneously drops to its accustomed octave (m. 64). It continues through similar changes before presiding over the conversion back to the A section, m. 76.

The reprise will restore the Bb bump in the ostinato; but we have just been hearing hints of it: in mm. 64–65 the G♯ nudges up against the A♯ that is introduced into the c♯ chord (first in inner-voice linear motion, then independently). Then starting in m. 72 the effect becomes explicit, the pair emerging as the exclusive melody of the concluding four bars of the section.

These details are worth noticing, for in the final A section this pair of pitches forms one more special moment. When the ostinato trails off in m. 81, yielding to a brief spell of suspended animation, its last utterance is the B♭–A♭ embellishment. Then the thoughtful little high treble solo comes in, and it starts from just this pair (with the B♭ nicely pinned for a moment). The two notes do absorb into the descending motion that follows out of them, but the quotation will seem clear in context if one tries playing m. 81 and just the first two high notes. They have emerged from the heart of the piece into a lighted, airy prominence.

At the very end the A♭ assumes a constancy that recalls its behavior in the B section. It keeps thumping to the last, and since the melody now slows up to whole notes, the A♭'s seem to have the last say.

The opening melody of the composition, after a rhythmically active fall through the triad, features a slow, scalar climb up to a G♭ that can link back to the starting pitch, to which it immediately turns. The melody then finds a medial position between the opening outer limits of F and A♭, the D♭ in the middle of m. 4. The settling is certainly transient, the phrase line carrying us right over into a repetition, and the ever-present bass A♭ weakening the brief sense of I_3^5 under the D♭. The connecting V^7 prepares a more convincingly root-positioned I in m. 5, and thereby suggests for the prior I the additional role of cadential $^6_4$. Both $^5_3$ and $^6_4$ interpretations are simultaneously possible because of the transient feel of the A♭, and the sense of cadence, now postponed, is further elided in m. 5. The dominant, meanwhile, is the site for the lazy septuplet that is so typical of the composer in this frame of mind.

The second time around, though, we get the same ambiguously inverted tonic chord, m. 8, beat 3; but the slur ends here and the chord remains for another beat, so we experience it in a more conclusive way, and the pair of phrases will bring the opening statement to a close. Throughout, the accompaniment has enriched the melody by doubling most of it at the sixth.

In m. 9 the quick change from dominant major to minor may foreshadow the parallel minor in the B section (see for example m. 43, with minor v). But the minor form at first serves as ii in G♭, given the V of IV that follows. But then reappearing in convincing fashion as a cadential $^6_4$ in m. 11, the minor dominant is installed as local tonic (m. 12), the focus of this second area of melody.

This region likewise proceeds as a double phrase; the second part sequences the tonality to b♭ minor, vi of the overall key: see the cadential $^6_4$ in m. 15. (The reharmonization of a tune segment in m. 14 points the way.) Both tonal areas in this interior period feature reinterpretations of the earlier prominent G♭–F, quoted in the original register: see m. 10, and then mm. 14 and 16.

In the returning primary D♭ theme, the septuplet is a touch more restless—and it will appear once more, at the end, in still more fully flowered form. The peak G♭ in m. 26 is this time unresolved: it does not fall back to the F which gives rise to it (and with which it has become associated in various harmonic colorings), but stands for the fully open dominant that leaves the A section hanging.

What resolves this, of course, is the parallel minor i that opens the B section. Actually, it takes a moment for us to fully realize this *is* minor music, for the first half-measure has no clarifying third. But the open fifth itself announces the ominous tone, and will be a vertical feature throughout. It is a little unclear which voice in the bass carries the growly tune—the moving part is at first the lowest notes, but we end up largely following the higher strand. (The frequent parallel sixths between them reflect those in the A-section melodic doubling.) The low positioning of the melody allows the unchanged ostinato to sound on top, in preparation for its emerging role in this section.

The whole aims toward the minor v (the a♭ minor tonicized in the A section), attained by m. 43 after the repeated half cadences on the open fifth; and the music starts up again, for an unusually lengthy exact repeat.

The wholesale softening we hear beginning in m. 60—a long way of bridging the expressive gap back to the tender A section music—introduces a series of beautiful suspensions (the first is the treble C♯, downbeat of m. 61). The suspension-prompted wandering of the ostinato figure, m. 63, is part of the trend. In m. 71, the surprise C♯^{7}, V^7/iv, is a welcome if momentary diversion from the steady emphasis on half cadence that has continued.

The returning A is very brief, almost a coda. The melisma that introduces the repeat phrase, m. 79, outdoes those earlier like figures. And the repeat itself lasts only a moment, being arrested by that sudden solo in m. 82.

The V^7 that enters after the solo indirectly retains the B♭ that ends the solo line (which has just outlined vi, deceptively resolving the V^7 before it). B♭, the framing pitch of the solo, is thus gently brought back down to the level of its origination in the ostinato. We gently focus the pure V^7 in the middle of the measure and more gently still move into I. The highest-line melody, now so very slow and perhaps no longer the focus of attention, is no more than G♭–F (twice, from m. 84 to the end), which extends, echoes, and calms the many stressed G♭–F pairs of the piece (dating back to m. 3). These 4–3 couples motivically imitate the ostinato's 6–5's together with the various outgrowths of that figure. And, as 2–1, the little hitch in the inner voice, m. 85, may contribute to this picture as well. As rest overtakes these features, their source, the ostinato itself, holds sway—the delicate heartbeat and energy line of the whole.

NOTE

1. One thinks immediately of the slow middle area of the Fantasy Impromptu—music in, by the way, the same key as this prelude. Both are ABA pieces that sectionally alternate parallel major and minor; in the Fantasy the mode and mood positions in the form are opposite to those in the prelude.

Prelude No. 16 in B♭ Minor

For all its surface bravura, this raucous piece may well disappoint. The relentless treble business, superimposed on a stubbornly unchanging bass gesture that outlines an unadventurous harmonic life, ultimately makes for a noisy assertion of fairly feeble ideas. Rather like an etude in its insistence on a single technical challenge, the piece makes none of the poetic discoveries offered throughout the companion preludes, and is one of the low points of the group.

The introductory dominant seventh, a bombastic presentation of the chord under a top line that connects chord tones F and C by passing tones, springs out first as V^9, the G♭ stridently applied as appoggiatura to the F. This G♭–F pair may pick up from the G♭–F that are the final two melody notes of the previous prelude (thus forming one of those precious links that join the preludes into their larger whole). If so, something soft and lovely has been taken up and spit back in anger.

The manner of this prefatory announcement is not heard again; the device is separate from the body of the piece, and starts things off obtusely. The styling that follows is then literally applied throughout, except for some focal moments. First, in m. 17 the bass pattern is broken and then withheld for a moment; what follows is thereby more clearly perceived and integrated as a reprise (at a higher dynamic level, and with buttressing bass doublings). A second break, in both texture and manner, occurs in m. 30, where the strummed chords increase the harmonic rhythm, which has not been faster than one chord per half-measure. This break, like the earlier one, has come at a cumulative V^7.

The flurry of two-handed sixteenths that follows seems an arbitrary change in the overall level of energy, which is in any case reconstituted in m. 34. Finally, the region from m. 40 to the end makes reference to both these brief medial changes—the quarter-note chords in m. 40, the two hands of sixteenths afterward, and the two final chords a quarter note apart. The basic gestural content of the music is thus abandoned toward the end, in favor of its exceptions.

An initial oddity is the grouping of bars by threes: mm. 2–4 are the i chord, mm. 5–7 the iv. After two more bars with one chord each, the rate of half-measure chord changes settles in as the norm, up to the half cadence at m. 17. The frantic rush of sixteenths above this, by turns scalar, sequential, cascading, and so forth, is hardly a melody, and is in any case too swift and jumbled to allow for appreciation of its details.

With m. 10, where progression in half-note amounts begins, we have the first of several sets of sequences that help to organize the busy surface; mm. 10–11 are transposed up a step, thus tonicizing c, in mm. 12–13. The c area is a passing region to III, which is reached in m. 14, the first of several important mediants. This III is also momentarily tonicized, but things turn immediately toward V for the half-cadence at the break in phrase.

In the strengthened repeat that begins at m. 18, all proceeds as at first until in m. 22 the B$\flat\flat$ turns the e$\flat$ minor (iv) into e$\flat$°. This will serve as (borrowed) supertonic for another move into III: the sequence e$\flat$°–A$\flat^7$–D$\flat$ over mm. 22–25 works as ii°–V^7–I in D$\flat$. The diminished form of the ii actually points to a local tonic *minor*, and in fact over the next two bars the III is altered to its minor form.

This in turn leads us further afield. With double common-tone link the d$\flat$ yields F$\sharp^7$ and thus the unlikely b minor (m. 28). (The d$\flat$, as c$\sharp$, acts as supertonic for b.) With the bass F as chromatic passing tone, the whole sequences down a step to a minor (m. 29). Thus the key has been sinking by whole steps, D$\flat$–B–A. But the a minor merely gets us, again by double common-tone link, to none other than F^7. This is the second focal arrival at V, m. 30.

The mediant is again passed through in the sequence of quarternote chords that follows. (This series of chords seems to review much of the harmonic life of the piece to date.) But the resumption of earlier manner in m. 34 restores the tonic. And in fact we are home for good—perhaps prematurely, given the noise the piece continues to make. For with the exception of a single iv, all chords from here to the end are tonic or dominant, apart from one sudden, brief departure. The continued surface agitation, lacking now any apparent motivation, seems superfluous.

The departure comes in m. 40. A new chord pops out unexpectedly, C$\flat^6$, certainly the N^6 of the key. Chopin lingers here for a while, in familiar fashion, and even momentarily tonicizes it: its own dominant seventh links a second C$\flat^6$ with a C$\flat^5_3$. But N will otherwise fulfill its usual cadential pre-dominant function; for the next harmonies are just the V–i succinctly forming the cadence. Intervening is only the last rush of sixteenths, which messily describes V anyway: F's, A's, and C's are the tones from which all the leaps are made, and on which all the appoggiaturas lean, nearly crushing the harmony beneath.

The sudden resumption of normal form in m. 34 after the four bars of arbitrary-seeming gestural departure may actually hinder the perception of some design in the piece: the music takes up its course by dropping us back to m. 10. As the earlier spot was driving toward the half cadence, the corresponding moment here approaches the full close.

Prelude No. 17 in A♭ Major

This is a very rich, generous composition, thickly spread with lux-urious inner-voice detail. Wide-ranging chromaticism due to sequencing and a basic format of full-fleshed, middle-register chords contribute to the overall lushness.

   The music opens with an accompaniment figure that will soon be surrounded by activity, but will remain quietly present throughout, welling up now and then to mark a structurally sig-nificant moment. As it swells and falls in initial solo, we must wonder if the $^6_4$ effect is illusory: perhaps we only await the sound-ing of the root note. Consider in this regard the opening of Schu-mann's song, "Ich grolle nicht":

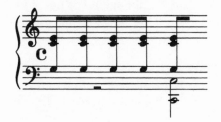

But though the length of the Ab^6_4, with its own finished dynamic curve, begins to convince us to accept it as just such a quasi-stability, we are about to encounter harmonies that will change that impression. The Eb^7–Ab that follow will join with the opening $^6_4$ to complete a full cadential pattern. When summarized as three successive block chords, the four-measure progression casts the first chord in a different light. The subtle contradiction between these two interpretations—of cadential $^6_4$ and of "rootless" $^5_3$—is a fine curiosity from which to set forth; and the issue will be joined further on down the road.

But the opening situation is more complicated still. Even before the resolving tonic of m. 4 has come into focus (at the middle of the measure, with the resolution of the Bb), we realize we are hearing not an Ab-major chord but an Ab dominant seventh. The first sound of the measure suggests a I chord in the making, if only the Bb, suspended indirectly out of the prior V^7, will give way to Ab; then the opening formula will be fulfilled. But immediately the Gb is added. It is as if we touch ground only to spring off on the first bounce.

This avoidance of I will continue throughout the opening period, driving the music onward to the end of a pair of matched phrases, where the full tonic is finally given.

The measure-long rising and falling reach of the motivic melodic curve (m. 3, m. 5 and so forth) imitates and fleshes out the swell of sound over the initial vamp. This arching gesture, together with the appoggiaturas both large and small (C to Db and F to G over the V chord of m. 3, the Bb to Ab of m. 4), adds warmth and detail to the rich musical fabric.

In m. 5 we have the IV that resolves the previous Ab^7. This IV is hesitantly established: it alternates with V for a while, two primary chords a step apart jockeying for position; the V^7 of m. 6, particularly, seems to retrogress to IV before finally resolving, deceptively, to F (m. 8). But again F is not vi in Ab, but rather an applied dominant. As in m. 4, the format provides a first moment when we think we have our simple vi, until the F–C span is filled in as $V^7/$ii.

The supertonic arrives, its own seventh pushing it right on to V^7, which, briefly touching base with I, returns as the stable, concluding chord of the opening phrase (m. 10). This half-cadence is marked by a measure of pure consonance—the first since mm. 1 and 2, which it clearly resembles, the accompaniment figure asserting itself now that nothing else is happening around it. (It is perhaps *more* consonant than m. 1, having none of the uncertainty associated with the $^6_4$ position; ultimately, neither moment is fully stable, compared with m. 18, which they both predict.) At the same time, measures of moving melodic eighth notes—mm. 3, 5, and 7—have each been followed by measures of two slower concluding notes, while m. 9 lands on a single, measure-long tone. The effect joins with the accompaniment condition to deliver all of the prior music into this point.

A thicker repeat ensues, certainly in search of the terminal I to balance this half-cadence. That I (m. 18)—the first proper tonic sound in the piece—exactly matches the V of m. 10, and finally resolves the issue raised by the opening $^6_4$. In fact, the residual accompaniment, after the downbeat, exactly quotes the music of mm. 1–2, which has thus acquired its missing root. The melody has been altered now to end 3–2–1, and the anticipating A♭ sixteenth note in m. 17 nicely clinches the moment.

A stunning change ushers us into the next phase of the composition. The melodic A♭ of the cadence is restruck and suddenly harmonized by a chord spelled here as E (with the A♭ as G♯)—this as a convenient form of F♭, the borrowed VI of the key. But, as has been happening several times already, with the accompaniment fill-in the chord is revealed as a dominant seventh, in this case of A (=B♭♭, the Neapolitan of the key). Extensive modulation by sequence, graced with rich inner-voice detail, begins here, and an earnest assessment of the harmonic activity is essential to appreciate the passage.

The rising chromatic bass in m. 20 delivers the A chord into an A-based Italian sixth. This resolves to G♯⁷ in m. 21, yielding the next sequence. The same connection is made at the end of m. 22, the last sonority (C, E, A♯) functioning as Italian sixth (inverted) for the B⁷ to follow. This then brings us back to E, the starting point and goal of the passage: the high melodic G♯ over it brings the initial G♯ (of m. 19) up an octave, and completes the cycle that first exposes ♭VI, the alternate key center in this piece. (The medial station of c♯ is to be understood then as d♭, the borrowed iv of A♭, as the harmonies of the parallel tonic minor are being explored.)

We can trace the high melody from here in chromatic descent (with minor interruptions): G♯–Fx–F♯–E♯–E (downbeat of m. 26). Then E is clearly installed in cadence, with the downbeat of m. 27 ending a full cadential formula. The rich sequential harmony accompanying the descent to this point is studded with augmented sixths: the E of m. 24 is filled in on the second eighth as German sixth, on the third eighth as French sixth, to the D♯ chord of the second half of the measure (the voice leading may be hard to follow on the page); the same situation obtains a step further down in m. 25; and finally, in the key of E, we have Fr^6, based on C, resolving to I$^6_4$ based on B, m. 26. (This delivers the cadential $^6_4$.) The concentration of harmonic change is very intense, with additional chromatic details deepening the color. But all finally settles down on the E of m. 27, for here is the format of resting familiar from the earlier cadences: E is presented in just the terms in which A♭ and E♭ had each been ratified. And E is now retained and confirmed plagally over a five-and-a-half-bar stretch. Its subdominant is a minor, not A major, so the plagal motions are modally mixed.

A very simple link brings us back home to A♭, and the restart of the piece. If we only change one pitch of our E-major chord, and change it by the smallest amount, E to E♭, we win back our tonic chord, in parallel minor (again, enharmonically). Hence E major becomes g♯ minor (m. 32), which is promptly respelled as a♭ minor (m. 33). (This continues the appeal to harmonies derived from the orbit of the parallel minor since this whole departing episode began. And the last-minute respelling verifies all the earlier enharmonic interpretations.) The next measure brings, again by double common-tone link, a d$^{°7}$ (sharing the a♭ and c♭ with the prior chord); this serves as vii$^{°7}$/V; the V, E♭^{7}, follows, and starts the principal music over again.[1]

The replay is much thickened and strengthened, and proceeds as far as the half-cadence at the end of its first phrase. At this point, m. 43, a new departure begins; and it, too, starts from E. Like the earlier alternate section, this area is rich in sequential repeats and in inner-voice passing detail (see, for example, m. 44), along with some luxuriant arpeggios (as in m. 43). The break from E♭ (V) to the key of E is sudden, and delightful: the pitch E♭ is reheard as the third of the new dominant, B^7 (where it is of course respelled as D♯); thus the root of the dominant in the main key is reharmonized as the third of the dominant in the subsidiary key.

The four-bar phrase, of simple harmony itself, is then sequenced up a whole step, in F♯ (starting in m. 47). (Two tones in common, B–G♯, link the E and the C♯^{7}.) In m. 51 we sink back to E for a moment—the bass motion in m. 50 has brought F♯ to F♯^{7}, leading in the B^7; and then sink further, in rapid sequence, into E♭ (m. 52) and then D.

Now this D will be put to very strange use. More inner-voice passing motion fills it in as a German sixth (downbeat of m. 54); but before this item can be resolved, the contrary motion lines first invert the chord (fourth eighth note, m. 54) and then expand it in such a way that, with the central two tones held in common (F♯, A), it suddenly is traded for an entirely *different* German sixth, the last sound of m. 54. This is the move that will bring us home, for the E♭$^6_4$ resolution of this German sixth will result in cadence on the E♭ that serves as long introductory dominant for the general return, m. 65.

The cadential $^6_4$ in m. 55 gives way to a colorful diminished seventh, embellisher of the B♭^{7} to come. This V/V then lands squarely on E♭ (m. 57), which now assumes the definitive stance of stability so well established in this piece.

Over the next five bars this E♭ will alternate with its own (borrowed) subdominant, a♭ minor. This modally mixed plagal stasis is of course directly reminiscent of that heard on E in mm. 27–31; and comparison of these two areas will confirm the E as the borrowed submediant of A♭, the upper-neighbor harmony to V.

There is now a protracted lull on the E♭. Certainly the introductory two bars of the piece are referred to, particularly in the dynamic shape over the four-bar equilibrium. The length of the moment is decidedly odd, but perhaps this much emphasis is needed to reabsorb and settle the various strayings up into (and beyond) E. But also strange is that the E♭ is a pure triad, not a dominant seventh; lingering so long with it, we may begin to accept it as having tonic stability.

But then our recapitulatory area begins, m. 65. This denouement features some very obvious changes that affect the mood strongly. First, the general sotto voce condition is a marked reduction of the buoyancy of the opening page. But that insistent and rather gross pedal tone, the repeated downbeat A♭ in sforzando, conflicts with the hushed tone. The first of these perhaps puts E♭ in its place. While the recapitulation is due to start on V⁷, after so many bars of stable V the downbeat of m. 65 otherwise needs to assert the return to tonic plainly.

A♭'s are further struck as pedal tone in this first measure. The effect is to keep the chords above close to home, as if the harmonies associated with the opening section will no longer be given free rein. In this spirit, the A♭ chord of m. 66 is devoid of that original G♭, the note that added instant life and predicted early adventure in m. 4. This I, no V⁷/IV, is tamed. (But other, comparable alterations in this area are less clear in their intent and effect.)

The first phrase comes to its usual half-cadence in m. 72; and the repeat phrase begins. At its end, m. 80, the melody lands on $\hat{3}$ in place of the $\hat{1}$, suggesting the extension of cadence to come. And the positive quality of the normal authentic cadence of the original is replaced by the regretful mood of a modally mixed plagal form: the sequence is d♭–A♭ in mm. 79–80, instead of what otherwise was to have been just E♭–A♭. Of course, this iv–I effect is copied from the earlier such progressions built around E and E♭, and again these three key regions are associated, and their mutually acting status in the whole further confirmed. Indeed, the plagal formula is repeated several times now, as it had been in the other areas.

The cadence region then extends, in part due to the ambiguous condition of the tonic chord. Again like the opening measures, and indeed in actual quotation, the A♭ chord acts like a stable harmony, but also partakes of the provisional quality of cadential $^6_4$. Adding to the ambiguity is the echoing presence of the sforzando A♭'s.

The last of the alternating iv's goes into I in m. 83, and, with one more melodic segment left, the pattern suggests another switch to iv before settling on the downbeat I that will finally coincide with the loud bass A♭ and complete the cadence of the piece. But no iv intervenes. The result is a curiously flat cadential arrival, no approach chord ushering in the downbeat tonic. We are left with the lingering $^6_4$ converting directly into $^5_3$. It is as if, at what is set up as the point of arrival, we are forced to realize that that arrival has already taken place (one measure earlier).

The repeated 3–2–1 figures come to rest here as well, with the anticipating A♭ announcing the formal downbeat representation of $\hat{1}$. But with no chord change before the bar line, this arrival must take effect without the standard support of a harmonic change *back* to I—which thus is already present, if in compromised form. This is the start of the ultimate terminal first degree of the piece, and its installation is remarkably inert.

A final, coda-like area now follows, the tonic note repeated with chordal fluctuations underneath. The chord that alternates with I, a ii^7 over an E♭ pedal, suggests both V and IV (the subdominant now normalized). By m. 86 it is purely V that alternates, but with the A♭ above continuing as treble pedal there is still the lack of a dominant-to-tonic movement. Even the last breath of V at the end of m. 87 is constricted by the A♭ nearly above it.

The deep A♭ is struck like one more bell, and the gentle patter over it is just the $^6_4$ portion of I that formed the opening sonority, now, of course, with its root in tow. But here the pianist is faced with a problem: at the very last moment a little flurry in the melody, that upper-neighbor D♭ (perhaps one last feeble reminder from the dominant that never had its proper say), will certainly smudge the tonic chord, so that if the pedal is down, keeping the deep A♭ as root under the quotation from m. 1, the fermata at the end will retain the D♭ along with the tonic chord tones. But, on the other hand, if the performer deftly raises and reapplies the pedal, so as to eliminate the D♭ from the final sound, the bass A♭ will be lost as well, and we are left with—precisely—that initial tonic $^6_4$. This time we would certainly take it as a root-position form missing its root—which, however, is not the note about to be sounded below (as in the Schumann example) but rather the one just recently sounded, that last in the series of assertive bell tones. One is reminded of the slow movement of Beethoven's Seventh Symphony, where the opening event is a sustained, ambiguously intended tonic $^6_4$, a sonority that returns intact as the final sound of the movement.

NOTE

1. Curiously, this precise series of connections, in the same key, is found in the slow movement of the "Pathétique" Sonata of Beethoven. The principal theme is in A♭; the second theme, in a♭, finds its way to E major (as ♭VI); and the way back to the beginning is found in the emergence of d^{o7} from g♯, to act as leading-tone diminished seventh to V.

Prelude No. 18 in F Minor

There can be little doubt that this is the weakest of the preludes. It barely comes across as a composition, in that its elements—themselves ill-formed—do not seem "composed" into an arrangement of any satisfaction. The piece presents a short list of items clumped into locally cohering successions that relate to each other in only the starkest ways, without true forward motion. By the time the piece is over, nothing seems to have happened; the cadence just puts a stop to the noise.

The individual gestures are actually ugly. The unapologetic minor dominant ninth in m. 1 seems spat at us, and is made even more unappealing by the interference of the stressed passing F above it (which barely gives way to E in time). The sixteenths that lead to the chord unconvincingly assert g°–ii° in f—because the C and A carry so much weight. Perhaps the initial C/D♭ pair predicts the strident verticalization of those notes in the chord. In any case, these initial two notes are directly lifted off the end of the previous prelude; the change of mood could not be more succinctly stated.

When in m. 3, after the opening group has been forced at us a second time, the sixteenth figure grows out of bounds, the lack of any texture beyond the octave doubling that will be a constant feature throughout precludes any development of detail or depth, and seems an indication of true creative fatigue.

These continuing rapid notes apparently aim at describing more of the dominant (according to the endpoints of step segments, the notes left by skip, and so forth). Thus, the progression has so far run ii–V, with i expected eventually. This tonic is supplied by the sequencing up a fourth of the original complex. The sixteenths spill over into the new repeat, with an alteration in the early part of the measure (the figure seems to start late and is consequently cut short) that results in the vague presence of the F chord in the sixteenths themselves—that is, prior to the pair of chords they presumably aim to introduce (according to the model of m. 1).

Due to sequence, i is actually bypassed, the F-based chord already acting as dominant ninth to iv. This chord continues on in the rush of notes that extends the sixteenth-note activity, and reaches a defiantly blunt statement of resolution in the stark 2–1 figure (on B♭) in m. 9, a resolution then spat back out at us on the second beat. The added sixth that makes the chord even more unpleasant to hear suggests that it can simultaneously be considered as ii^7 (with G as root): and so it acts, for the next two chordal items are vii$^{\circ 7}$ and i, the f of m. 11 finally representing the tonic. Thus, the music has avoided i in its reach out toward iv, which arrives in a form that twists us back toward i. These chords continue to come across as so many slaps to the face, and are interspersed with the same noisy octave sixteenths that play out the prior chord and then unceremoniously plunk down the top note of the next one.

The following chord, b$^{\circ 7}$ in m. 12, resolves in the nondominant (common-tone) fashion, to the A♭, m. 13, and a new surface behavior abruptly begins. The A♭, III, is in a functionless $^6_4$ state, consistent with the unstable and restless quality of the music so far. The bald octaves that follow may again recall the C/D♭ pair from earlier on.

The next sputtering turns A♭ into A♭$^+$ (m. 14), which, in resolving to f in m. 15, can also be taken as C$^+$, the augmented V. The pushy chords that follow are familiar sonorities, but oddly treated.

A♭^{7} and e$^{°7}$ both resolve to a D♭ (the diminished seventh by the common-tone resolution); the D♭ is VI, and its power to resolve its own dominant seventh is diluted by the interpolated chord, as well as by its own inversional status. The g^{ø7} that comes next (beat 4) restores an earlier sonority; but its status as ii in the key, like that of the VI before it, is vague, given that the feeling for f as a key has barely been established so far.

The sequenced chords of m. 16 crash down on B, m. 17, which further confuses any sense of progression. This turns out to be the start of the large sonority on the next beat, a strangely voiced augmented sixth (Italian at first, German by the time the cascade adds the A♭'s). This inverted D♭-based augmented sixth points to a C-based resolution, and thence to f for cadence. But the process is abbreviated here, with f baldly arriving in the furious trill, no C having intervened as mediator.

The cacophonous figure after the trill is in shape reminiscent of the e♭-minor prelude, and doesn't succeed in contributing to any confirmation of the f—it just sounds like bass noise in a crunched linear pattern. Its component chromatic descents begin at steps above pitches of the tonic sonority needed for cadence, but there is no clear aim. The falling off at A♭ after A yields an uncertain tonic flavor, with the C at bottom suggesting $^6_4$ (or a bare V).

The long silence that separates the piece from its terse cadence can almost suggest a distancing from the music so that the closing formula can pretend to resolve what has not been set up as requiring resolution. It is as if the cadence aims at erasing the piece that precedes it. But the jarring sound of the fff open-fifth dominant rings true with all that has gone before.

Unpleasantness certainly has a clear place in the literary and visual arts; its purposeful occurrence in music is much rarer, and puzzling. Consequently, one must wonder if this prelude would meet even its own composer's approval. Perhaps the hasty and unreconsidered product of a fit of ill temper, the piece conveys a blatant but rather immature anger. One is tempted to picture the composer temporarily resentful of the self-imposed obligation to write a thoroughly new piece in each next key; perhaps having run out of steam on one day, he seems bent on making us suffer for it. The result comes at us with a force due only to loudness and speed. Hearing it is like receiving a beating.

Prelude No. 19 in E♭ Major

The great registral dispersal of the light, rapid triplet-eighths in each beat produces a marvelous buoyancy in this piece, a delicate surface again remarkably different from anything else in the collection. The first of each three treble notes being highest in a fixed pattern, we easily sense the melody riding in quarter notes over the puffy accompaniment. Thus, for example, the melody starts by rising in a large, airborne tonic triad, before turning down by step.

Generally these melody tones are grouped in threes—m. 2 repeating m. 1 an octave higher, m. 4 sequencing m. 3 a perfect fourth lower—or in double measures (mm. 5–6 vs. mm. 7–8, for example); and the rate of harmonic change is similarly timed. But two parallel exceptions to this format occur at critical points in the composition. Starting in m. 29, the melody forms a sequence of rising thirds. The unit of sequence is two beats long, and so the music seems suddenly to move in two-four meter (across the notated three-four). This hemiola effect is supported by the harmony, which likewise changes every two beats over this same stretch of time. The result is a compression of the "measure" into two-thirds of its normal length. The music speeds up, not by an acceleration of its beats, but by a faster rate of "downbeats."

The point is, this propulsion is aimed precisely at the break in m. 32, the only such moment in the piece. The arrival is at V (thinly outlined), and the midpoint of the prelude. A formal reprise follows.

The normal rate of harmonic and melodic progress is restored now, but hemiola is encountered once again, starting in m. 65. Here the melody consists of a two-beat alternation between E♭ and a series of tones that fall into a line of steps. (The harmony remains on the tonic chord throughout.) This compression, then, complements the earlier one by ending the second half of the piece, and by resulting in the punctuating tonic statements that balance and formally resolve the medial V.

As the piece begins, we quickly discover that chordal sonorities are constantly enriched by the pervasive use of suspensions, pedal tones, and the like. In the first two bars, on I, each beat presents the chord purely, which will be a model for many beats. But in m. 3, on the other hand, an E♭ bass pedal tone underlies the progression $b^{\circ 7}$–A♭–$d^{\circ 7}$ (with the diminished seventh as embellisher of the IV). In m. 4, the resolution of the $vii^{\circ 7}$ to a vi is only apparent, with the C's as suspensions. Similarly, the dominant is reached at the downbeat of m. 6, but its full realization is delayed by the suspended E♭ and the leaning G. In such ways the chordal connections—here from V/V into V—form a smooth, nuanced continuity.

The melodic particle G–F at this point echoes those notes from the higher octave at the crest of the opening arpeggiation (end of m. 2). As the current segment of melody now repeats, the G–F element recurs, m. 8; here the V has its seventh added, in preparation for return to I at the second start in m. 9. (The two-voiced neighboring in the preceding V/V—the treble D and the bass B on beat 2—is typical of the fluctuations in the chord presentations; in this beat only three of six notes are actually of the F^7.)

The restart proceeds nicely halfway (through m. 12); but a surprise turn is encountered on the downbeat of m. 13, with the German sixth on C♭. Along the path from here to the emergent V at the midpoint of the piece, the surface of the music continues on with only the details of harmony and voice leading varying to produce change and forward motion. These then must be noticed attentively.

A first such detail involves the resolution of the German sixth, which ought to be to B♭, but in m. 14 is g (iii⁶, V/iii, iii), substituting for the V. (The respelling of G♭ as F♯ at the end of m. 13, after the chord has been prolonged through the bar by melodic neighbor-note motion, can alert us to the change.) Thus, the bass C♭ does move down to B♭, but this pitch is neither the root nor the fifth of the resolving chord, as is usual, but the third. The move is comparable to the substitution of g for B♭ in a deceptive resolution of an F⁷, and, like such a substitution, it is temporary: for B♭ does arrive following a bar of its own dominant, and it does so just in time to form the end of this second eight-bar stretch. (Again, the downbeat bass B♭ in m. 16 lays out the V; the rest of that beat is suspended F⁷, with the full V given on beat 2.)

Colorfully, this dominant spontaneously turns into its minor form at the end of the measure, as a link to the next area, an eight-bar phrase that will begin to repeat in m. 25 but, halfway through, switch into the hemiola region that yields the ultimate V. The melody of this new phrase derives from that of mm. 5–6, plus the original rising arpeggio figure.

The minor v, meanwhile, is consistent with the chromaticism of m. 13 (since German sixths are built out of borrowed ♭VI). But it will serve to introduce G♭, borrowed ♭III, the focus of the new phrase: D♭⁷–G♭ follows, with the b♭ of m. 16 acting as iii for the following V and I of G♭.

After four bars of this material on the borrowed mediant, the G♭ emerges as the basis of a new German sixth: the added F♭, for G♭⁷, is respelled as E in time for resolution to the F-based B♭⁶₄. Full arrival into B♭ is then achieved. As before, the details are worth noticing: the B♭-centered progression from m. 22 runs I⁶₄–IV (over F pedal)—embellishing °7–V⁷–I.

In a replay of m. 16, B♭ again converts to b♭, and the previous phrase begins over. As noted, it proceeds only four bars, at which point all of the foregoing functional harmony, based on the large-scale move from ♭III to V, is derailed by the hemiola area. The melody note that starts m. 29 is the expected one in the repeat (see downbeat of m. 21); but the chord supporting it is a diminished seventh, derived by double common tone from the previous G♭

chord (sharing B♭ and D♭/C♯). If the function of this chord is—suddenly—unknown, nothing is clarified as we move every two beats to a new diminished seventh, each one a whole step higher than the last. These then simply pass the ball, until we reach one that acts with functional intent: the final diminished seventh, rooted on D, is the one that, as vii$^{\circ 7}$ in E♭, is functionally equivalent to B♭, V. The conversion takes place, and the passage abruptly stops. The oddity is that the dominant chord that ends all of the previous ambiguity is itself so weakly stated; as a mere shell, it is less certain than the diminished seventh it replaces. And yet this is the dominant that we must relate to the ultimate tonic at the end of the other period of hemiola.

The entire piece begins afresh now, and follows normally through m. 43. Here suddenly the familiar melodic turndown G–F comes out as G–G♭, and a new succession of diminished sevenths begins, again proceeding in rising bass whole steps, but this time changing every beat. (It also moves by falling treble half steps, these two conditions simultaneously possible according to the unique geography of the diminished-seventh sonority.) The entry and exit of this chain of diminished sevenths resemble the earlier passage. The first diminished seventh emerges from the I chord before it by common tone (the embellishing function); the following ones are passing chords, suspending any sense of function and key until the last one, e$^{\circ 7}$ at the end of m. 44, acts with direction as vii$^{\circ 7}$ of the next chord, which is a long, definitive ii. This chord, lasting three measures, will initiate cadence: in m. 46 it is intensified as ii^7, which gradually gives way to V as its suspensions dissolve over the course of m. 48, and then to I. The prominent F/G pairing over the ii in m. 46 revives the cresting pair (most recently of mm. 34–35), and there is even the octave-reduced echo, two bars later, familiar from the earlier high points.

The pedal E♭ that begins in m. 49 indicates the arrival into essentially cadential tonic: in fact, a coda-like area follows from here. In the melody that plays now, the alternation of C♭ (mm. 49 and 57) with C (mm. 51 and 59) as upper neighbors to B♭ in corresponding moments yields a trading of the modes that is a linear residue of the significant harmonic modal borrowings earlier on.[1] Subtly sewn into this melody is a quotation of the beginning of the piece, at m. 53, a climb through the I chord ending in the G–F turndown.

The G^7 that harmonizes the G/F pair here casts it in a light different from all of its other, variously harmonized, occurrences. This
applied dominant resolves on the third beat; but over the next two
measures the same three-note melody unit is twice sequenced
down, and here the harmonic rhythm is different—the applied
dominant is a ^{o7} (as vii^{o7}/V), and we wait *three* beats for its resolution. The quicker chord change in m. 54 is a hitch in the predomi-
nant harmonic rhythm, and the next time around, in the large
repeat that starts in m. 57, this same spot will bring a much
stranger twist. For the G/F pair in m. 62 is given the same support
of G^7, but the next harmonies are of E and A. This is a puzzling
moment; the E^7–A couple neither follows the G^7 in any progressive sense nor bears any functional status in the key of E♭. The best
that can be said is that the first of these two chords shares two
tones with the G^7, and then pairs up with the second one to harmonize the treble passing tone E. It is as if a wholly foreign
thought intrudes but is promptly discarded. For the A root is then
recast in a^{o7}, which, as vii^{o7}/V, restores the harmonic sense. V is
achieved by the end of m. 64 after the first beat suspensions (over
the B♭) and the intervening tonic $^6_4$. I then holds, to the end.

This is the site of the second set of hemiolas, which will act as a
stretto into the final pronouncements of I. Its pairs of rising notes
in the melody echo the similar form of the earlier hemiola melody,
while the slower, descending chromatic line that alternates with
the E♭'s recalls the melodic moment at mm. 43–44. The melodic
aspects of the two spells of diminished-seventh harmony are thus
combined in this closing gesture.

NOTE

1. For a similar alternation of C♭ with C, see the long grace note figure
at the end of the composer's E♭ Nocturne, Opus 9, No. 2.

Prelude No. 20 in C Minor

The funereal majesty in this celebrated prelude is softened to a hushed mourning in the second four-bar phrase, which itself is then echoed at a distance for a third, final area. The punctuating last measure of whole-note tonic otherwise distinguishes as cadential the last phrase from the middle one.

The first measure presents a key-defining progression, i–iv–V–i. Only the tonic chords are pure, both subdominant and dominant containing extraneous tones that absorb by step into consonance in time for the statement to round back to i. The extra note in the iv is the E♭, suspended out of the i chord. Outlasting the iv, it persists into the V (yielding a momentary augmented triad). It finally gives way to resolution in the D sixteenth note, doubling at the third the melodic fall to F, chordal seventh that continues the dissonance of the chord after the suspension has resolved. The rhythm of this resolution then becomes a constant feature, recurring in each measure until the final chord.

This opening progression supports a melodic move from $\hat{5}$ to $\hat{3}$. In the next bar the melody is sequenced to move from $\hat{3}$ to $\hat{1}$, which would complete in two stages an unfolding of the tonic triad. But the next to last step, as D♭, is wrong, describing a Phrygian arrival into C. But by this time C is barely heard as melodic goal, since the harmony has undergone a reorganization away from c. We may be tempted to think of the D♭ chord in m. 2 as N in c; but the following E♭^{7} (the C in it is a passing tone) sways us toward the tonality of A♭, and the whole measure is to be taken as I–IV–V^7–I of that key. Thus, the progression of the opening measure is sequenced onto the submediant level; and the melodic D♭ in m. 2 is a *normal* passing tone in that key. The end of the piece will correct this situation: the harmony will admit a D as passing tone there, and proper scalar arrival into C will be achieved.

Meanwhile, m. 3 aims back at the original key focus, with the G^7. But the next chord is not c but C^7, V^7/iv. The iv that follows features the sharpest expression of the rhythmically active dissonance, which occurs now in the highest voice as an extruding appoggiatura indirectly suspended out of the prior chord. (This same effect will be felt in the next bar.) The push into iv—which thus has bypassed the tonic—is promptly cancelled by retreat to i.[1] And then the drive is on toward V, for a half-cadence that ends the entire four-bar span. (The slurs and the crescendo indicate that after the measure of VI the motion should reach in a single gesture toward the concluding V, but, given the tempo and the weight of each chordal attack, it may not be easy to project this intention.)

More than just dynamics change as the second area of the piece begins. The thinner chords and higher registration help to lighten the tone. But a subtler change takes place: in the first four bars the melody is undoubtedly on top, with the inner voices distinguishing themselves only when they contribute dissonance to the chords; while now an inner line suddenly blossoms into our notice. The tops of these chords will yet emerge as the melody, but for the moment these move without creating interest; meanwhile, the next-lower succession, starting G–A♭, draws us in. First of all, this line starts by actually quoting, in register, the original melody of the piece, as if the true melodic line is to be shifted to this position. Second, the rhythmic activity occurs only in this voice now. And at that point this line works against the harmonies in a very

notating a minor chord here. As E♭, the melody seems at odds with itself within the measure. And, indeed, the next measure, which echoes this one, presents beats 2 and 4 with an unchanging chord supporting an unchanged melodic pitch. But on the other hand, if for this reason we allow C on beat 4, it too will seem odd—is it still V/iv, as in beat 2 (in which case it does not return to iv), or just a major form of tonic? (It could even be construed as IV/V, partaking of a IV–V–I arrival into the G cadence. This interpretation would fit with the larger drive towards half cadence indicated by the two-bar slur and long crescendo; but it is hard to hear after bars 1 and 2 have conditioned us to take fourth beats as closing off their measure's progression.)

Prelude No. 21 in B♭ Major

As has been so before, our attention is at once divided between a leisurely melody and a very much more active accompaniment. Contrary-motion lines in the bass of m. 1 gradually unfold a tonic B♭ chord: the F initiates passing motion both down to B♭ and up to D (across the gap). Thus, a space defined by the B♭ chord is drawn out from the F after the chord has been stated in outline on the downbeat. At the same time, these lines work together to suggest a harmonic progression within the basic I. If we start by identifying F^7 by its distinguishing tritone E♭–A— especially as these notes join with the sustained treble F—then a small V–I motion is heard into the following attack. The C's that come next—again, with the F above—continue the fluctuation, with another V–I pair across the bar line. In this vein, after the first two eighths have outlined the I, the E/G pair can suggest V/V as it moves to the V. Measure 2, by way of lines that still delineate intervals of I, presents a similar progression. Then, from similar lines, such local progressions can be detected thereafter, transposed to nest within the larger, full-measure harmonies as they progress through the piece; for example, as organized within c, ii, in mm. 3–4.

The larger shift from I to ii takes place under the melodic D that closes the neighboring begun on the previous downbeat. This suspends the D out of I, but, oddly, there is no resolution to a chord tone of ii, and the resulting configuration perhaps suggests IV^7 at first, until the bass details, and of course the entirety of the next measure, show otherwise.

The ii yields to V in m. 5 under more active melody, and this is the site of a first element of modal mixture, the G♭ appoggiatura to F in the high bass. This pitch, which takes its cue from the passing chromaticisms in the earlier bars, initiates a styling that will come to dominate much of the piece. As a lowered sixth degree protruding out of the V chord, it clearly invokes the parallel minor (b♭) scale. G♭ is similarly exposed in the full chromatic passing motion in the lower voice, where it hesitates across the bar-line gap before continuing on down, and these passing G♭'s produce a first impression of borrowed harmony, the local IV (on beat three) replaced by iv (within the underlying two-measure V). At the same time, the new, twisted shape for the upper accompanimental strand will also exert a strong influence later on. Meanwhile, V finds its way into I, and the manner of the beginning is fully restored as the phrase comes to an end.

Although the flow of notes continues as before, the pace of harmonic progress quickens, as the basic chords change now every measure. A clear IV begins m. 11, as introduced by its own dominant—although the bass details again suggest ii, to which the IV in any case moves in the next bar. V is the goal of the region, as pronounced on the downbeat of m. 13. At this point the accompanimental matter fully takes over, emerging into the forefront in both registers—an interesting development in terms of our divided attention at the very outset. The initial form is that of m. 2, doubled at the octave. At the end of the first measure the chromatic descent in the lower part continues past D, through the D♭; this replaces a I with a i, and more modal mixture, as inspired by m. 5, will follow. In fact, the accompanimental shape in m. 14 more resembles that of m. 5, of which the prominent G♭'s are reminiscent. The immediate A♭–G♭ descent here can be traced back one step to the B♭ in m. 13 (beat 3)—thus a descent in the b♭-*minor* scale. And if we isolate and follow the lower chromatic descent from m. 13, we will find it breaks the chain of half steps only at C–B♭, which characterizes B♭ as a first degree. The modal mixture continues with the pairing of IV and iv at the end of m. 14—again a product of the bottom-line descent. And these local harmonic effects have our close attention, since as a consequence of the accompanimental surge the larger level of harmonic flow has temporarily halted.

This outburst gently subsides, dynamically and registrally, into I, until the higher octave duplication drops off, and the original locus of the piece is regained. The chromatic descent has stopped, and the modal mixture with it—I is not paired with i in mm. 15 and 16.

But then ♭VI suddenly breaks out—a grand flush of harmony from the orbit of b♭ minor just as the modal mixture seemed to have been contained. The G♭ root will steadfastly hold the harmony for a full sixteen bars, in a giant magnification of the original G♭ of m. 5, that first seed of modal mixture as nurtured along by the mixture that has been emerging since. Strikingly, this VI does not take part in progression: it almost comes to seem like a new tonic. First, there are eight measures of the static harmony, underlying an unhurried melody that is new only to the extent that it varies and then grows from the original theme (compare the shape and rhythm of the first five pitches here with the opening group). The accompaniment adds interest with the gently undulating neighbor motion, in a repeating pattern of four notes that just echoes, in rearrangement, the start of the melody it accompanies (or, for that matter, the original melody shape itself). This pattern fills only two beats—against the three-beat metric still enforced by the melody; thus, while hemiola is not achieved, we do have a fine situation of crossed meters, with the two parts coming into realignment every six beats.

When next the melody repeats in echo, the G♭ chord has prominently gained a recurring F♭, which renders the whole a dominant seventh. Thus the status of the chord is left in further doubt, as it can no longer be considered either a VI or a new I; and as the repeat is to be a full one, this G♭^{7} will last an unusually long time for an unstable chord (and a functionally ambiguous one at that). We are obliged to rest with it, waiting to hear where it will go. Meanwhile, the accompanimental pattern, changed to echo the melodic falling thirds even more clearly, still argues with the three-four meter.

In m. 32, after the melody has come to an end, the accompaniment changes slightly to emphasize the F♭, which now occurs on two successive beats. Its respelling as E at the last moment indicates what is about to happen, for the G♭⁷ resolves after all this time as an augmented sixth—to F, V. (The two leading tones to F—E and G♭—jump widely to find the resolving octave.)[1]

By the time m. 33 is over we discover that the F is for the moment not root of V but fifth of I_4^6; and that a kind of reprise of the opening theme begins here. But this return is of a special sort. Its tonic chords are all in second inversion, and a tense F pedal underlies it all. Leading to a climax in m. 39 that subsides into a quiet root-position tonic and its placid aftermath, the reprise is really a single, enlarged cadential $_4^6$ pointing at cadence, taking its outward form from the opening music. In this scheme, what may strike us as a "middle section"—all that which occurred between the original music and its restoration—has really been a one-chord preparation for that return. These two extended chords are obviously matched in their amplification, and we come to realize how uniquely this piece creates form. After the initial exposition of tonic theme that concludes in m. 16, the G♭ chord already lays the basis for the German sixth that yields the return. Its static presentation suggests its unitary purpose and nature, and although the reprising aspect of the music that follows fosters the apprehension of a concluding ternary form, we must come to regard the "B" and "A" of ABA each as essentially single, local details represented in augmentation as "sections." These attach to what would then appear to be the "body" of the piece, the first sixteen bars, and form the beginning steps of cadential process for that body.

At the start of m. 33 a full beat of four-register F starkly resolves sixteen bars of G♭. Then, as the accompanimental lines try to assert I, the powerful F enforces the $_4^6$ condition. The recapitulating area then prolongs this tension, which mounts toward m. 39. It has made no pretense of reestablishing and starting out from a stable I, the $_4^6$ standing in place for the tonic of m. 1. The melody above this is a rising sequence, in stretto, of the original first two notes, the falling third F–D, repeated here as, again, the first two downbeat notes, supported by the I_4^6. Over the F pedal this figure is succeeded by the step-higher G–E♭, and then by A alone and by B♭, two pitches that advance the upper note of the falling third, as the pace of sequence is doubled. The larger harmonic sense can again be referred to the applied details within, and moves through ii (c, supporting the melodic G–E♭, mm. 35–36), iii (d, m. 37, to support the A), and IV (m. 38), all over the F pedal and all leading to the F in m. 39. Thus the harmonic rhythm speeds up to keep pace with the contraction of the melodic sequence unit.

The melody notes interact with the accompaniment in a vital way here. Now the accompaniment is in two-register form, as in its solo moment. So the melodic D of m. 34 seems handed to us at the top of the accompanimental step line in the previous measure. At the end of m. 34, the D returns as the last accompanimental pitch in the treble, which separates from the bass so as to reinforce the melodic link from the previous downbeat to the coming one. The same things happen with E♭ in m. 36. Then in m. 37 the last treble eighth is F, which is actually the expected next downbeat melody pitch: so that the full figure in the sequence, A–F, is heard after all, but in diminution. Then m. 38 treats B♭–G♭ the same way. The effect is experienced as follows:

The melodic compression, the larger progressing harmonies, and the organizing F pedal beneath all culminate in the downbeat F of m. 39. The last sound before it is the triple-octave G♭, a striking intensification in the accompaniment that yields the clear succession G♭–F, ♭$\hat{6}$–$\hat{5}$, into the downbeat—again G♭ as the representative of modal mixture. Strangely, the F is not really clarified as V: is it still I$^6_4$? In fact, full V doesn't arrive until all the energy that has been built up is spent—the modest last eighth of m. 44. Meanwhile, the fortissimo F is dramatically repeated in a taut and energetic alternation with e♭ minor, borrowed iv, the climactic triumph of the minor mode in this major piece.

The climax winds down by way of the meandering, crooked path of the accompanimental material, as in mm. 13–16. Again, the modes are mixed throughout, with adjacent I–i and IV–iv pairs, the descending A♭–G♭ link, and downbeat upper-voice D♭ and G♭, in addition to familiar chains of suggested applied dominants and the straight, descending chromatic scale that keeps the whole step only on B♭. At one point, in m. 43, the harmony drifts into an unlikely A major, an uninterpretable bypath. But all subsides into modally mixed cadence, iv–V–I, by the downbeat of m. 45, where the original registration is restored.

The tonic reached, the energy is spent. A thin shadow of the accompaniment is left, which forms the basis of an extended confirmation of the tonic. In m. 46 the downbeat F and following E♭–G♭ pair call back the great moment in m. 39, and the accompaniment billows once more, but pointing clearly at home. After these two bars are repeated, the solo eighth-note figure drops an octave, a further tapering off. The quieter, less active progression starting in m. 50 is a timid vi–I, but hinting at dominant flavor (in the coincidence of the bass passing tone A and the treble neighbor E♭). The vi–I pairing, perhaps a reflection of the rather odd G that vaults from mm. 46 and 48 directly into I, repeats, with then only the solo bass figure remaining in motion. In the bass repetitions[2] the last note is again G, from which the fall is made back to 1̂, in echo of the vi–I idea. (See in this connection the similar G's left hanging at the end of mm. 45, 47, and 49.)

But just as a state of rest seems achieved, a light flurry of energy emanates from the figure, which suddenly rises up in a twisted, sequential motion that seems to spring forth from the figure's half-step E–F. It reaches a lone, rather proud third degree, D. After a breathing space, this 3̂ will be heard to descend simply and confidently through 2̂ into 1̂, embedded in the declarative V–I formula that has really been lacking throughout, and that serves locally as a correction of the earlier, identically timed, weak vi–I's. At the same time, the padding above enforces a level of imperfect cadence, in keeping with so many of the other prelude endings.

NOTES

1. At the last possible moment the German sixth turns into a French sixth, a C replacing D♭ as one of the notes filling in the G♭–E augmented-sixth span.

2. Some editions omit a measure that repeats the bass of m. 53.

Prelude No. 22 in G Minor

The turbulence is more convincing in this piece than in the f-minor prelude. Contributing to the sustained effect are the strong bass melody doubled throughout in octaves; the closed, thick mid-register chords swiping at us from off-the-beat positions; and the multiplicity of diminished sevenths and other similarly cramped sonorities.

The bass melody starts by lifting the B♭ octave directly off the bottom of the sound just fading from the end of the previous prelude and delivering it by step into the new downbeat. When the G is reached and held, the bottom interval of the new tonic sonority has been delineated by this connection of the tonic notes of the two successive pieces—a fine instance of a frank link between preludes beyond the generalities of key and mood.

This brief outline of i is all that is offered by way of initial tonic; an immediate ii–V progression above makes of the bass G a suspension. V is replaced by the associated vii^{o7} in m. 2 (numbering from the first full measure); as this chord reappears in each of the two following measures, the preference for this sonority over the less aggressive dominant-seventh type is already evident. Its first resolution here is deceptive, to VI (the "embellishing" function); but at the end of m. 4 it resolves back to i, rounding out the opening presentation of the key. Throughout, the aggressive effect of the dissonant chords is advanced by the format, in which they pounce headlong on the second eighth note of the measure, and probably in sforzando (given the need to soften from them while remaining at forte).

In this same condition chromaticism leaps suddenly forth in m. 5. The E♭-major treble attack crunches against the bass C♯ to form a German sixth, inverted into the diminished-third position. The relaxation to V is normal, but instantly the progression is sequenced down a whole step. As the sequence is exact, the resolution is not to iv, but IV.

An octave-higher repeat of the first four bars begins with the pickup to m. 9. But m. 8 works oddly. The bass slur ends at the A, which acquires chordal significance due to its agreement with the treble and its additional separation from the G. Thus, the original introductory figure is reoriented away from i. Indeed, the early presence here of the next measure's ii°, which meets the bass F♯ to sound vii°⁷, compromises the description of a g-minor chord that is otherwise implied by the whole measure of bass melody.[1] In an ambiguous mix tonic and pretonic harmonies are presented simultaneously; neither chord seems to predominate.

Chromaticism in sequence follows the four bars of repeat, as was so originally. The new sequence, like the old, duplicates down a whole step; and further echoes are heard in the E♭ chord of m. 13 and the D♭ of m. 14, in reference to the first harmonies of mm. 5 and 6; similarly, the pronounced C♯ and B of the earlier pair of measures show up as the terminal bass notes of the two new sequence terms. But the bass melody is different; and the pacing of the treble swipes is doubled—a condition that will hold from here on. The unlikely succession A⁷–D♭ results when the transfer to the second transpositional level follows the unresolved second chord of the first sequence unit. In principle, the F that starts off the next term could suggest a d-minor chord is to follow, which would serve normally. Indeed, the similar G⁷ at the end of m. 14 does resolve properly, an alteration after the first note of the next measure allowing for c minor as a third link in sequence is begun.

The iv followed by vii^{o7} in m. 15 suggests a return homeward, but the harmony next takes an adventurous turn. Continuing bass chromatic descent, which can be traced back to the E♭ in m. 13, brings the A of m. 15 to A♭, which transforms the vii^{o7} into a German sixth, pointing at a G-based resolution. The downbeat of the next measure states the expected chord, but the German sixth returns promptly on the next attack, where it is spelled as a dominant seventh. Indeed, this A♭^{7} yields the notable D♭ that emerges at the bottom of the chromatic bass line. These last few chords are rather too compressed in time to be fully grasped. But the A♭^{7} leaves its impression over the remaining bass notes; as a second-eighth hiccup, and in its cramped inversional form, it rings true in this piece. (In fact, the $^4_2$ inversion is intervallically equivalent to the form of German sixth found in mm. 5, 6, and 7.)

The arriving D♭ is an unlikely chord in the g-minor environment, although it did sound briefly in m. 14, and is further reflective of mm. 6–7. It must strike us as functionally obscure until it proceeds into progression. But in short order chords of E♭^{7} and A♭ confirm it as IV of A♭, and for four measures we settle into the Neapolitan region, momentarily tonicized (by now a feature of the preludes). In this temporary stabilization, the bass runs descending scales from D♭, diatonic versions of the prior chromatic scale. But these are not D♭ scales, but A♭, running from $\hat{4}$ to $\hat{4}$. The effect helps deflect any serious focus on A♭, which only weakly achieves root position.

At the bottom of the second scale, D takes the place of D♭, but a sequential shift *down* a step—by now a familiar device in this piece—is launched. As the music is lowered from its temporary A♭ focus into g, the functional value of A♭ as the N region is confirmed. The sequence is not exact, either harmonically or melodically. The bass scale, now of g, runs from C to B♭, and is gapped. An F still starts the top treble line, but F–G–A♭ is tightened up to land on the new tonic note. The iv in the latter half of m. 20, always an easy move from N, sets up the return to g; the apparent d^{ø7} may just start the D^7 (to follow iv, and lead to i): it has the D and C, and the F and A♭ are on their way to F♯ and A.

The restored key is confirmed by the straightforward i^6–VI–ii^{ø7}–V^7 that follows. But just as it is to resolve into tonic $^5_3$, the music suddenly jumps back and repeats the entire sequential area.

This produces the unlikely succession D^7–D♭. After both terms of the sequence, the firm progression is played twice (starting in m. 31), with the end of the repeat altered to allow the opening music to start up one last time. In a sense, the music has been driving towards cadence since the emergence of N in m.18. With each failure to complete (after mm. 24, 32 and 34) a doubling back leads to a new attempt. Perhaps then, the reappearance of the theme here represents a more determined regathering of force, as if to get a running start from further back.

Although the propelling qualities of the music have continued unabated, extra momentum is gathered toward the end as the original phrase snags on its second measure; the repetitions trap the vii^{o7} in its deceptive resolution to VI. The tension increases under the accelerando and the octave rise of the treble. The VI that keeps tripping things up in the drive toward tonic has actually sneaked in as substitute for i at the end of m. 34, over the introductory 3–2–1 bass figure. The only way out seems to be explosion, as the VI breaks out of all bounds to crash squarely on the downbeat—in defiance of a sternly enforced, piece-long ban—where it is joined by the bass C♯ to form one last German sixth. This moment stands for so many of the sonorities in the piece, but most precisely that of m. 5, which recurs here grossly enlarged.

Both space and time dramatically separate this chord from its resolution. That even so forceful an outburst can be so handily contained, with a sharp dispatch by the rhythmically virile cadence, attests to the vigor with which the high energy level has been asserted throughout.

NOTE

1. This harmonic reinterpretation of the B♭–A–G closely resembles the situation of the bass 3–2–1 figure in the b-minor prelude, mm. 2 and 8.

Prelude No. 23 in F Major

Filigrees of trills and rippling arpeggiations compose the airy texture here, reaching to a precious delicacy through a series of transpositional shifts upward.

The plan of the piece is simple, compact, and expertly turned. The four-bar theme presents a tonic chord and then immediately flips it over into a cadential $^6_4$ that proceeds directly into cadence. The opening tonic is colored with a continually added sixth, the D's acting as recurring appoggiatura to C (in two registral positions). The tonic $^6_4$ lasts through most of m. 2, giving way to V only on the fourth beat. Cadence is reached on the following downbeat, and then confirmed in local V–I gestures. These settle into a full bar of I, in m. 4, with swirls of doubled neighbor tones providing a light embellishment.

This concise theme is then transposed in a block, up into the dominant key. But a simple twist in its last measure is crucial for the remaining course of the piece. The consequent of the cadential formula in m. 6 is the C of m. 7, alternated as local tonic focus with G^7. But in m. 8, in what ought to be its stablest pronouncement, the C emerges as C^7, due to the late entry of a single B♭. Thus C is turned back to its original status as V of F. And this dominant seventh just points to a third presentation of the little theme, once again in the tonic, and again shifted higher in registration. This proceeds normally from m. 9 into m. 12. Meanwhile, at the end of m. 8 some treble D's appear as steps related to E's; these both recall and prepare the similar flavoring by D of the opening measures.

The next movement onward takes place by way of m. 12, where the concluding tonic behaves just like its counterpart in the previous theme version: that is, F, as I, is inflected into dominant-seventh shape, now pointing toward IV. This treatment of the true I is less routine than the parallel case with the earlier, temporary I: hence perhaps the composer's accent on the unexpected E♭, which again single-handedly does the job.

What is suggested, of course, is a fourth round of theme, yet higher, and now in B♭. But just when the piece is on the point of becoming too literal, as the B♭ version starts up in m. 13, a transformation takes place. By the start of the next measure it is apparent that the theme is not continuing. Instead, the first-measure upper part is successively repeated within chord changes that in fact form the cadence of the piece. The measure of false start in B♭ is the central detail in this development. As a B♭ chord with added G's it has been fully prepared by the harmonic gesture of m. 12 (including the G's already serving as added tones there), as well as the familiar styling of the basic chord of each theme statement. But in the next measure the sound of G^7 puts a new slant on the prior combination of major triad with added sixth, which can also be heard as a minor-seventh chord—in this case g^7, as chromaticized into G^7, or ii^7 becoming V^7/V, in preparation for cadence.[1] In this regard, the apparent switch to root position as g^6_5 gives way to G^7 seems to serve notice of the emerging harmonic direction.

The V^7/V moves to a V that takes shape very gradually, over the course of mm. 15 and 16. In m. 15 the low C–G lays out the makings of it, but F is prominently suspended throughout the measure, and A curiously alternates between motivically standard upper step to G and independent arpeggiated tone: so that the measure is as much F^6_4 as C. (The D's, also left over from G^7, are now just steps to C.)

The downbeat of m. 16 rolls out a clearer C^7. There are still the suspended F's, but all other tones are now either of C or step-related to it. If the F–to–E move in the left-hand part promises a fully realized C^7 at last, there is then the exposed A that follows. Oddly, the notation presents this pitch as the end of a line—thus as unresolving. But it will readily be heard to absorb into the flow of sixteenths at the G that occurs in the same register on the next beat—that is, exactly when and where its resolution is expected. (The lack of any notational indication of so unmistakable an effect is puzzling.) The fourth beat then contains only tones of C, and the hard-won dominant is in focus. The emergence of plain V on a fourth beat makes this point of the cadence resemble the corresponding point in all the earlier phrase cadences (beat 4 in mm. 2, 6 and 10); and in fact the perceived connection of the left-hand A to the G a beat later just quotes the prominent falling whole step that sounds in the lower-staff part at each of those points.

Cadence on I occurs with the next downbeat. The arriving tonic is extended, expressed and confirmed in the most natural manner—as one final full theme statement in the key of I, now in the tinkly regions of the instrument. The stretch of small V–I alternations is extended to become a route of registral reduction, until the original site of the music is restored.

Measure 21 would seem to call for an unexceptional arpeggiation of I, a final settling of the postcadential V–I fluctuations. But a celebrated surprise is in store, for as the unfolding rolls out—now devoid of any linear tones—the insertion of a single E♭, accented for emphasis, recasts the entire final sonority into a dominant seventh. To make sense of this bizarre twist we need only refer back into the piece it ends: for twice before we have heard the concluding tonic of a theme statement turned into a dominant seventh. Indeed, the last version in F ended this way precisely, with F^7 emerging from F (m. 12).

The effect, if not actually to suggest yet another theme statement, at least recalls the earlier, similar expectations. The hypothetical repeat would be in B♭, the version that never did materialize.

Of course, no shift into IV follows. The fermata, though written over F's only, captures the entire pedal-sustained sonority, which then must be accepted as an oddly flavored tonic chord, perhaps gesturing out beyond the piece, while also reaching back as an echo. For a terminal chord it is of course absolutely exceptional for the time and place of the preludes.[2] But in addition to the specific logic that justifies so unusual an ending for this particular composition, there is the history of imperfectly resolute cadences throughout the preludes, including now this latest example as a most special case. And if there has always been another prelude to continue, there is yet one more now—if not by way of specific answer to this call.

NOTES

1. See, for example, mm. 5–6 of the first prelude for the same progression, ii^7 intensified into V^7/V.

2. But it would not surprise in a composition of the present century, when the lowered seventh, at least since Debussy, may serve to color a major triad without signalling the directional intent of the "dominant seventh" formation. Consider, for example, the second piano prelude of Gershwin, where at last touch a minor seventh is blended into the final tonic chord.

Prelude No. 24 in D Minor

Although not at the top of the small list of disappointments among the preludes, this last piece, if found lacking, will not leave the best impression of this splendid collection. The relentless bass pattern, itself an awkward formation, underlies a piece otherwise marred by an unimaginative literalness. For example, as the first harmony remains unchanged for the opening nine and a half bars, the accompaniment figure is played nineteen times in exact repetition. Similarly, a full fourth of the total span of the piece, mm. 19–37, is given over to a wholesale replay of the first eighteen bars in transposition. The spectacular scalar and arpeggiated runs quickly lose their impact through overuse; and the funeral bell that tolls so starkly at the end may impress more as a clumsy cliché than with real drama.

The long opening stretch of tonic harmony and the somewhat developmentally treated theme it supports set forth the key without exploring it. When the chord finally alters—to G^7 in m. 10—it is in the service of a tonal shift to F, which is reached in cadence at m. 15. The G^7, sharing D and F with the prior d chord, works as

V/V for F; the cadential $^6_4$ to which it moves gives way to the local V, C, gradually over the course of the next three measures: though the bass in mm. 12 and 13 is mostly of C (with suspended F), the F chord persists as a straight arpeggiation in the melody (in a figure imitative of the opening melodic gesture[1]). The measure of grand scale is finally full dominant, with the scale itself rushing headlong into the cadence point.

F as key focus is just a stage on the way to a, the site of the long repeat. Thus it is no sooner reached than abandoned: the bass F immediately underlies a French sixth that points to the cadential $^6_4$ for the coming a-minor cadence. Interestingly, the treble C–A–E starting in m. 16 directly imitates the treble F chord in mm. 12–13, but here the outlined triad is anticipatory rather than suspended.

The arrival into a is composed to resemble the earlier landing on F. Once again there is the rising scale and the halting of the melody. The additional flurry of rapid notes, in m. 17, sets the precedent for later figures. The F added to the a$^6_4$ there, as frank dissonance, is also predictive.

Once a minor is established, the accompaniment holds time for two bars—twice as long as the comparable moment for F in m. 15. This lends a the status held by d in the opening period of accompaniment, and stabilizes it as the larger goal of the key changes. The entire tonic triad has now been unfolded as keys, with the defining fifth, D–A, formalized as the sites of the two full theme statements.

Further key shifts up by thirds are entailed by the repetition, which must bring us from a through C (m. 33) into e, downbeat of m. 37. The linking detail into the last key, at m. 34, is not this time French sixth (as in m. 16), but applied ii^{ø7}. Also, a rerising arpeggio, in place of a scale, aims directly into the point of cadence.

The continued advance of key, though fully predictable, has lessened the overall structural impact of the original d–F–a series. The keys generated out of the triad of the second theme statement—a, C, and e—have been superimposed, amounting now to a proliferation of brief set-downs. Although the formal process ends here, in search of the original tonic the music will touch down twice more, on c (m. 39) and on D♭ (m. 43), both moments marked by false theme starts. The eventual goal, at m. 51, will be proclaimed by the theme in octaves, dynamically strengthened.

Meanwhile, the wandering is interesting, in the manner of a development. In the brief thematic quotations the basic arpeggiations downward and back up are followed, in m. 41 and again in m. 45, by a turn that resembles a later segment of the original tune (see m. 9, E–D–A as turndown from a rising triad). The shifting focus of tonality is likewise typical of developments. A bass move from E to E♭ stretches the received e minor of m. 37 toward G^7 in m. 38, for the piece of theme in c. A shift to the VI of c, A♭, yields the dominant for the next key moment, A♭^{7}. The statement in D♭ seems fairly stable—the chord lasts for four bars; but in m. 47 the advance of A♭ into A, in both the melody and the accompaniment, produces an unstable D♭$^+$. This lasts for four more measures, and comes to serve as a kind of leading-tone chord for the arrival into d: at the last moment the D♭ is respelled as C♯.

The oddity here is that the D♭$^+$ chord already contains two tones of the d it moves to, and this blurs the distinction between approach chord and goal, thus blunting the force of arrival. In a sense, the D♭ since m. 43 has been a stably harmonized leading tone. From there to m. 51 this chord is gradually transmuted into d, first with the raising of its fifth and then with the raising of its root (the third being already present).[2]

The restoration of the original theme and key is at once directed toward the formal cadence of the piece, which will be achieved in m. 65. Expanding from the ii$^{\varnothing 7}$ of m. 53, a grand German sixth (at ff) introduces the cadential $^6_4$ two bars later. The bass note will be A from here to the point of cadence, and thereafter D until the end. The triple forte, treble octave doublings, reckless septuplets, and stretto all crudely reinforce the drive toward cadence. A ii$^{\varnothing 7}$ rides over the dominant pedal starting in m. 61, and full dominant is reached halfway through m. 64, just before closure.

A coda-like area confirms the tonic. The three remaining cascades all contain tones at odds with the bass chord—a gesture of dissonance found also in the earlier versions, at mm. 17, 35, and 36. Measure 66 presents a wide diminished seventh embellishing the surrounding i's; but the treble falls along a route of G^7 (with the E's as passing tones), which differs from the bass in one element. The figure of m. 68 repeats the diminished seventh but then the descending chromatic passing tone B♭ makes of it the German sixth that had preceded i$^6_4$. Here it reabsorbs directly into tonic $^5_3$.

As the entire sequence repeats, quintuplets are introduced (m. 72) to push to the end. The seemingly endless bass thunder comes to a halt at last, and the final cascade, on i with added step B♭, bottoms out on a 3–2–1 arrival into the tonic bell that rings with all of the finality missing among the earlier prelude endings.

NOTES

1. The theme of the D♭-major prelude is also echoed in this figure.

2. If the respelling to C♯ suggests the leading function of dominant harmony, we can recall that the resulting F⁺ triad, which of course is also the D♭⁺ triad, is just as well an A⁺ chord, V⁺ of tonic d.

For Further Reading

Because of their central place in Chopin's work and the comparable stature of the composer in the romantic period, the preludes are everywhere discussed, and descriptions of their historical context and meaning and of their style are found in all general music history texts as well as in essays that accompany score editions and recordings.

The starting point for the more serious student of these pieces must be the Norton Critical Edition of the score (W. W. Norton, 1973, edited by Thomas Higgins), which surrounds an authoritative printing of the music with a variety of information that ranges from textual notes and performance advice to "appreciations" from famous people. There are, as well, high-level analytic investigations of two of the preludes (nos. 2 and 6). Also included is a brief bibliography, which refers the reader to the basic historical and biographical accounts.

In 1975, Professor Richmond Browne announced the formation of an ongoing forum on the Chopin preludes to appear in the journal *In Theory Only*, commencing with volume I, number 4, which also included a penetrating article by Charles J. Smith, entitled "On Hearing the Chopin Preludes as a Coherent Set." The issues that followed for several years offer a fine opportunity to engage the preludes both singly and in groups from many points of view.

Otherwise, and in parallel to the widespread availability of the historical information, detailed analyses ranging from passages to full individual preludes are ubiquitous, regularly appearing as examples in music theory textbooks, as subjects of journal articles, as matter for argument in dissertations. The ongoing production of studies of individual preludes, together with the very occasional book-length treatment of some aspect of the entire group, can thus be explored in the standard scholarly sources such as *The Music Index* (1949–) or the *Répertoire International de la Littérature Musicale ("RILM")* (1967–)

About the Author

JEFFREY KRESKY is Professor of Music at William Paterson College. He is the author of *Tonal Music: Twelve Analytic Studies,* as well as articles and reviews for professional journals. As a music theorist, his interests center on criticism and analysis. He has also written four novels, as yet unpublished.

WHEN ANDY'S FATHER WENT TO PRISON

WHEN ANDY'S FATHER WENT TO PRISON

Martha Whitmore Hickman

Illustrated by Larry Raymond

ALBERT WHITMAN & COMPANY, NILES, ILLINOIS

The text for this book is set in Fritz Quadrata.
The illustrations are pencil and dye.

Library of Congress Cataloging-in-Publication Data

Hickman, Martha Whitmore.
When Andy's father went to prison /
Martha Whitmore Hickman :
illustrated by Larry Raymond.

p.   cm.
Rev. ed. of: When can daddy come home? © 1983
Summary: When Andy's father is sent to prison
for robbery and the family moves to be
near him, Andy is afraid of what the kids
at his new school will think.
ISBN 0-8075-8874-1
[1. Fathers and sons—Fiction.   2. Prisoners—Fiction.
3. Moving, Household—Fiction.]
I. Raymond, Larry, ill.
II. Hickman, Martha Whitmore, 1925-
When can daddy come home?   III. Title.
PZ7.H53143Wg   1990   89-77318
[E]—dc20   CIP
                                                AC

Text © 1990 by Martha Whitmore Hickman.
Illustrations © 1990 by Larry Raymond.
Designer: Karen Johnson Campbell.
Published in 1990 by Albert Whitman & Company,
5747 Howard Street, Niles, Illinois 60648-4012.
Printed simultaneously in Canada by
General Publishing, Limited, Toronto.
Printed in the U.S.A. All rights reserved.
10 9 8 7 6 5 4 3 2 1

Andy Wilson was feeling very grumpy and sad. He was also feeling very scared.

Tomorrow was his first day in a new school. He was starting second grade.

Andy had moved here in the summer, with his mother and his little sister, Angela, so they could be near his father.

That was part of the trouble about school. Sometime in the first few days of school, somebody was sure to ask about his father.

It might be the school nurse asking for his father's place of business.

It might be his teacher, asking get-acquainted questions— "What does your father do, Andy?"

Maybe someone he'd just started to be friends with would ask, "Where does your father work?" or even, "Does your father live with you?"

For a time it might be all right. He could say, "My dad makes furniture," or, "My daddy's going to night school. He's learning to be an electrician." He wouldn't be lying. His father *was* doing those things. But if they asked some other questions, he'd either have to lie or tell them, "My daddy's in prison. We moved here so we could visit him."

In Martinsburg, where they'd lived before, he didn't have to say anything. Everybody knew. It had been in the paper.

Andy was five when it happened. At first his mother didn't tell him. "Your father's on a trip," she said one morning when his daddy wasn't there. But one of the big boys on his street showed him the newspaper picture. Andy could see a man getting into a car with a policeman. The picture was gray and fuzzy. It didn't look like his father. "That's not my daddy!" he said.

"Oh, yes it is. Don't try to get out of it," the big boy said. "Your father robbed a warehouse, and he's in jail! Go ask your mother!"

He ran inside. "Mama! A picture a boy showed me—Daddy's not in jail, is he? Mama?"

"Who told you that?" his mother asked.

"Jimmy Sullivan. He had a picture—"

His mother started to cry and took him on her lap. "Andy," she said, "It *is* your daddy. His trip was to jail. I was going to tell you—"

"Jail!" he said. "Why's he in jail? When's he coming home? He didn't do anything wrong!"

"I'm afraid he did," she said. "Looks like he broke into a warehouse—with two other men. They stole some televisions."

"We already have a television!" Andy said.

"They were going to sell them. He thought he needed money to buy things."

"For us?" he asked.

"I guess so." She shrugged her shoulders.

"But when is he coming home?" Andy asked again.

"I don't know." His mother put her arms around him. "Not for awhile, I'm sure."

Things were different after that. His father was never there to read him stories or play catch in the front yard. His mother was often cross at him and Angela, and sometimes just sad. Arthur and Lewis still came to play, but his other friend, Donald, never came anymore.

One day Andy called him up. "Donald, can you come over?"

"No," Donald said.

"Why not?"

"I just can't," Donald said. "My mother won't let me. She said your father is a no-good criminal."

"Oh." Andy hung up and went to his room and lay down on his bed. His stomach felt funny.

When his mother called him for supper, he didn't go down. She came looking for him. "What's the matter, Andy?" she asked.

"Nothing," he said.

She sat by his bed a minute, then went downstairs.

One afternoon, soon after he turned six, Andy's mother took him to visit his father. First they went into an office. It was dark and full of desks, and everyone was wearing a uniform. His mother talked with a woman at one desk. "This way," the woman said, and she led them both into a small room. They held their arms out while she felt down the sides of their bodies to see if they were hiding anything in their clothes.

Then they went to a door, only it was a big gate made of white bars. A man pushed a button, and the gate slid open with a loud clang. They went through and started down a hall. The gate clanged behind them. At the end of the hall was another gate and another man in uniform. He pushed a button, and that gate opened, too. They went into a big room with rows of blue chairs and people sitting and talking.

"We'll wait here," his mother said, and they sat down next to the wall. "He'll come through that door," she said, pointing.

A door at the far side of the room opened, and a man came out wearing gray overalls and a gray shirt. His face looked almost gray, like his clothes. It was his father!

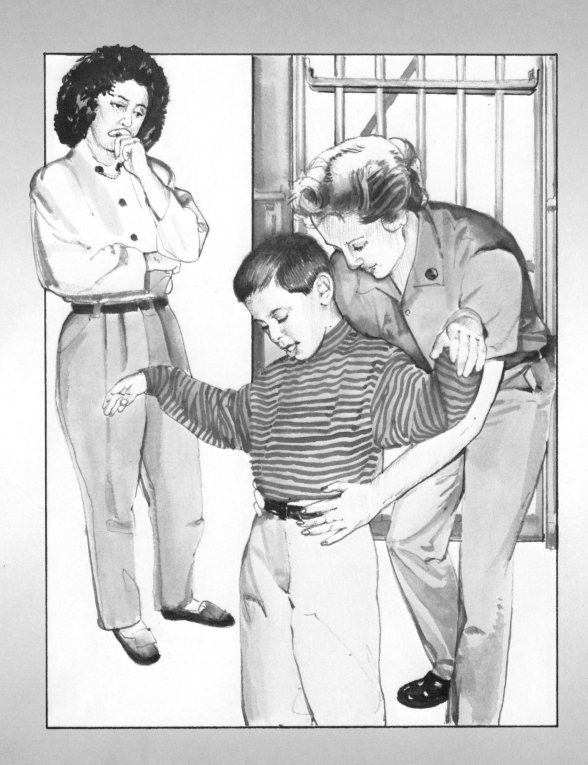

His mother stood up. Andy kept sitting, holding onto the edges of his chair. His father came over to them. "How are you, Andy?" he said. But it was as though Andy were company or they didn't know each other. His mother gave Andy money for the candy machine, and he went and bought a chocolate bar. He came back and sat in the chair while his mother and father talked.

After awhile his father said, "How are things with you, Andy?"

"OK," he said. He wasn't going to tell them anything.

"Anybody giving you a hard time?" his father asked.

"Nope," he said, and twisted his candy wrapper around and around.

"How's school?" his father asked.

"It's all right."

"Your friends coming over?"

"Sort of," Andy said.

His father looked at him for a long time, and then he said, "Andy?"

"What?"

"I'm sorry—for the trouble this is to you."

Andy started to cry. His father's lip twitched, and he looked as if he might cry, too. "I'm the one who made the mistake," he said, "not you."

Andy sniffled. "When are you coming home, Daddy?"

"I don't know. We'll have to wait and see."

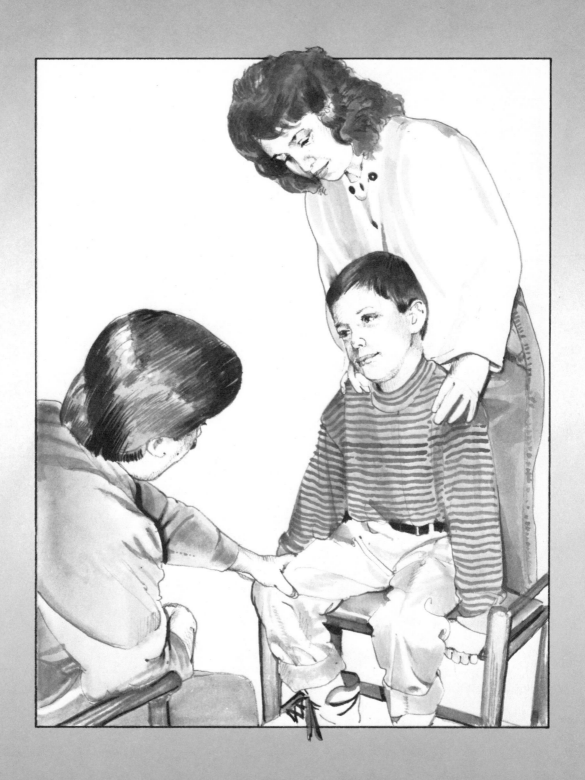

When Andy was six and a half, his mother told him his father was being moved to the state prison in Nashville. "He got three to ten years," she said.

"What does that mean?" Andy asked.

"They had the trial. He'll be in prison at least two more years. It could be a lot longer."

"Two more years!" Andy ran upstairs and threw himself face down on his bed. He heard his heart beating against the mattress. *Two more years!* he thought. *I'll be eight and a half by then!*

For several months he didn't see his father at all. Once in a while his mother would go on the bus to Nashville and come back the next day. His father wrote him letters. On Andy's seventh birthday, his father sent him a card he'd made with a picture of a boy blowing out seven candles. There were other people around the table, too, but you couldn't tell who they were—his mother, maybe, and Angela, and some other children. But nobody was big enough to be his father.

He showed it to Lewis. "Didn't he send you a present?" Lewis asked.

"He can't exactly go to the store and go shopping, Dodo," Andy said.

"Oh, I forgot," Lewis said.

That was one difference between Lewis and him. He'd never forget.

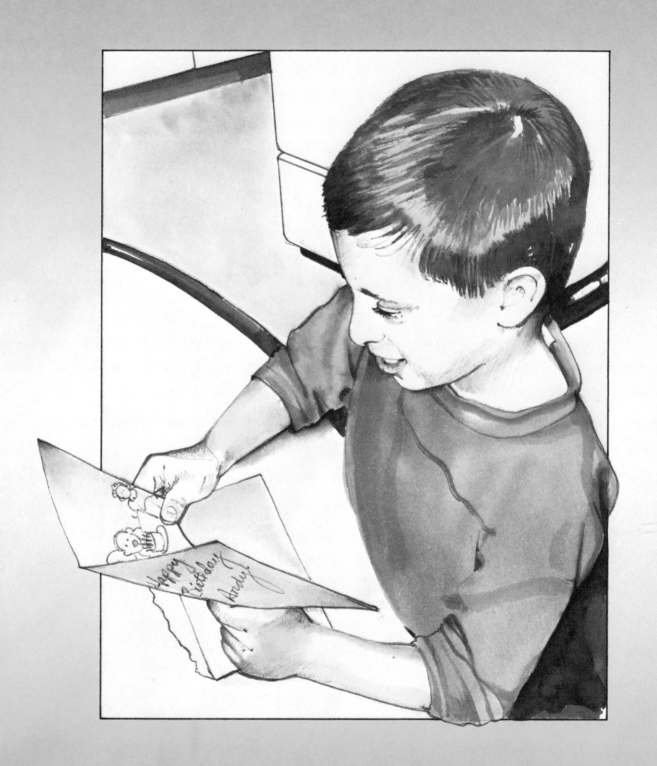

Early in July, when his mother came back from visiting his father, she said, "We're going to move to Nashville. I found us a place to live, and I know where I can get a job. We'll move next month."

Andy wasn't sure he wanted to move. He wanted to see his father, but he was used to Martinsburg. And what about school? What about making new friends? Would the kids be like Donald? What would he tell his new friends about his father?

They did move. Andy missed his friends, especially Arthur and Lewis. But he was glad to see his father again. Every Saturday, he and his mother and Angela took a picnic and went out to the prison. They'd go to the checkpoint—a small building where they signed up for the bus that would take them to the picnic grounds. They'd ride on the bus, and his father would come through a door of the prison and out to meet them. They'd talk and have their lunch and sometimes read together or play games.

Other families were there, too. Sometimes Andy played with the other children. One boy said his father might have to stay for thirty years. Another child's father was supposed to get out next year. It was nice playing with the other children. He didn't worry what they'd think about his father.

But when school started . . . *that's* what was scary. People were sure to ask him about his family.

On the first day of school, nobody asked.

On the second day, nobody asked.

But on the third day, the class started talking about families. Miss Quimby said, "I know some of you boys and girls have moved this summer. Why did you move? Let's start with Joel."

Joel was a boy one row over. Andy liked him. They'd played ball at recess yesterday, and he'd even been thinking of asking Joel over to his house. But he didn't know Joel had just moved here—they hadn't talked about that yet.

Joel seemed scared. "We moved from Little Bend," he said slowly. "We moved in July."

The teacher nodded pleasantly. "How many are in your family, Joel?"

"Well, my mother and my two brothers. And my father." Joel was glancing around the room, but he wasn't looking at Miss Quimby. Then he turned toward the window.

Andy thought suddenly, *Maybe Joel's father is in prison!*
Other families must have moved to be near the prison, too.
Was Miss Quimby going to make Joel tell about his father if he
didn't want to? Andy was frightened for his new friend. And for
himself. What would he say when Miss Quimby got to him?

"I see," the teacher said, smiling. "Thank you, Joel. Who else
is new—Sarah Jane?"

Sarah Jane stood up. She said that her family had moved
from Washington, D.C. Her mother had a new job here, and her
father was looking for a new job. They came just in time for
school to start.

Then another girl started to tell why she moved and who
was in her family. But Andy wasn't listening. He was sure Joel
must have moved here to be close to the prison. If he and Joel
could be friends, things wouldn't be so bad. Even if Miss
Quimby called on him, it wouldn't be so scary now.

But the bell rang before she got to him. The class went out for recess, and he waited for Joel by the door. "Hi," he said.

"Hi, Andy." Joel still seemed scared.

"You want to play Zimbo with me?" Zimbo was a game Andy carried in his pocket. It had little balls that rolled around on a flat circle with holes.

"Sure."

They went and sat on the steps. Andy gave Joel the first turn. "I just moved here, too," he said.

"How come?" Joel asked.

Andy swallowed hard. "We came so we could visit my father," he said.

"Is he in the hospital?" Joel asked. "Is he real sick?"

Andy felt his heart drop. He'd guessed wrong! "No," he said. "Is yours?"

Joel nodded. "He's very sick. They had to cut off one of his legs. Maybe they'll have to cut off the other one." His chin shook a little, and his eyes filled with tears. "We don't know if he'll get better."

"Oh," Andy said. He felt kind of sick to his stomach. He looked at his own legs and said, "I'm sorry, Joel."

"Yeah." Joel brushed his cheek with his sleeve. "What about your father?"

For a second, Andy hesitated. He wasn't sure whether to tell or not. Then he said, "My father's in prison. We moved to be closer to him."

"Oh," Joel said. "What'd he do?"

"He robbed a warehouse." Even now, he hated saying that. He hated hearing the words out loud, hated that his father had done such a thing. But Joel didn't turn away or even make a face.

"I met another boy whose father is in prison," Joel said. "I guess a lot of families come here."

"I guess so."

For a while, they didn't talk. Andy watched while Joel tilted his hand one way and then another to make the balls go in the holes. "Almost," Joel said, shaking it and starting over. "This is a neat game."

When the bell rang for the end of recess, Joel started to hand the game to Andy. "You can keep it this afternoon," Andy said.

Joel smiled. "Thanks! I'll give it to you after school. Wait for me, OK?"

Andy nodded. "I'll wait."

The next Saturday, Andy's family took their picnic again and went to the prison. Andy looked at it all in a different way now. It was awful having his father here, not out in the free world like he should be. But he thought of Joel and Joel's father.

"Dad," he said when they were all sitting around the picnic table, "when you get out of here, we don't need anything we don't have—right? We have what we need—right?"

His mother and father looked at him. "What's got into him?" his mother said. "What're you talking about, Andy?"

"Nothing," he said. "Just stuff . . ."

"Whatever we have will have to be enough. I'm through with stealing," his father said. Then he asked, "How was school?"

"It was fine," Andy said. "I was scared at first—" He stopped. He didn't want to tell his father he had been afraid of what people would say.

But his father already knew. "Were you scared people would stay away from you . . . because of me?"

"Yes, I was," Andy said, surprised. "But they didn't. Bad things happen to other people, too."

"Well, listen to him," his mother said. But she smiled when she said it.

His father was looking at the gates and the barbed wire and at the huge barred windows of the prison. "It's lousy here," he

said. "But some don't have anyone visit them. Week after
week—nobody. My family comes to see me." He turned to
Andy. "You stay out of trouble, Son, you hear me? I don't ever
want you having to come to a place like this."

"I don't plan to, Dad," Andy said.

"Nobody plans to," his father said. "You've got to plan *not* to."

Andy and Joel became good friends. Each Saturday Joel visited his father, and Andy visited his. Joel's father didn't seem to be getting better. One day the boys were talking about Nashville and how long they'd stay.

Joel said, "If my father gets better, we'll be here a long time. If he doesn't, if he gets worse and . . . " He looked up, his face sad. "If you don't see me here someday, Andy, then you'll know."

Andy nodded, feeling sorrowful for his friend. Then he said, "I guess we'll stay until my father's paroled. He has a hearing sometime this year. I'll get to go. He could be out in six months even." He didn't let himself think about it too much for fear it wouldn't come true.

The last Tuesday in February, Andy didn't go to school. It was the day of the Parole Board hearing. His family went, all in their best clothes. They passed through the clanging gates, but this time they were taken up a stairway and into a long room with a table and a lot of chairs. Two men and a woman stood at the other side of the table. Then Andy's father came in. He was dressed in his best clothes, too. They all sat down. The men and the woman asked his father questions and talked to each other. Finally one of them said, "Mr. Wilson, we're going to release you on parole, effective April tenth."

His mother and his father turned and hugged each other. Then his father hugged him and his sister and hugged his mother again. He shook hands with the two men and the woman. This time, when he went back through the prisoners' door, he turned and waved. "See you Saturday!" he called.

PAROLE BOARD

On the way home, they stopped for ice cream. Andy's mother sang all during the rest of the trip. It seemed to him she sang all evening. At night he heard her in her closet, rummaging in her clothes. She was still singing.

The next morning Andy went to school early. When the bell rang, he went in and got very busy making a calendar for March and April. He drew all the weeks and days with his ruler and a pencil. He wrote in the numbers, using a big calendar on the front wall that had all the months, so he knew which day to start on. When he got to April 10, he drew the one and the zero in great big letters. He took some gold gummed stars he'd brought from home and put a whole circle of stars around the day.

He didn't notice that Miss Quimby had come to stand beside him. "What's that for, Andy?" she asked.

"It's for my father," he said. "I'm making it for him. I'll take it out next Saturday. Did you know my father's in prison and he's getting out?"

"I did know he was in prison, Andy. I'm happy for all of you that he's getting out. It'll be like a party, won't it?"

"Yes, ma'am!" he said. Suddenly, he thought of Joel. He'd wanted to tell Joel. He started to look over to the first row. But he stopped. For a moment he was scared—maybe Joel wouldn't be there. But he was.

"Joel!" he called in a loud whisper. "My dad's getting out—April tenth. You can come over!" He thought again of Joel's father. "You'll be here, won't you?"

"Wow!" Joel smiled. "I think so, Andy. I think I'll be here!"

"Well, you come! We'll have a party when my dad comes home!"

Martha Whitmore Hickman wrote this book after a friend who works in corrections said, "We need books to help young children who have a parent in prison. Would you think about writing one?"

WHEN ANDY'S FATHER WENT TO PRISON is Martha Hickman's tenth book for children. She is a native of Massachusetts and has four children. She and her husband live in Nashville, Tennessee.

Larry Raymond earned a B.S. in Art Education and taught for four years before becoming a graphic designer and illustrator. His experiences in teaching young children as well as raising his own two sons have offered insights into the emotions he portrays in his realistic illustrations. Larry Raymond's work has appeared in numerous children's books, magazines, and corporate publications. He lives in the Finger Lakes region of central New York State.